The Grumpy Old Git's Guide to Life

The Grumpy Old Git's Guide to Life

Geoff Tibballs

Michael O'Mara Books Limited

First published in Great Britain in 2011 by
Michael O'Mara Books Limited
9 Lion Yard
Tremadoc Road
London SW4 7NQ

Copyright © Michael O'Mara Books Limited 2011

A CIP catalogue record for this book is available from the British Library.

Papers used by Michael O'Mara Books Limited are natural, recyclable
products made from wood grown in sustainable forests. The manufacturing
processes conform to the environmental regulations of the country of origin.

ISBN: 978-1-84317-583-4

19

www.mombooks.com

Cover design by Design 23
Designed and typeset by Design 23

Printed and bound by CPI Group (UK) Ltd, Croydon, CR0 4YY

CONTENTS

INTRODUCTION

Once men reach a certain age, in addition to starting to lose their hair, they also start to lose their carefree nature. Perhaps it's the realization that they finally have to start behaving like adults but almost overnight they transform from irresponsible teenagers into curmudgeonly old gits. Everyday gripes that were previously dismissed with a relaxed shrug suddenly irritate them beyond belief. They have enough pet peeves to fill a zoo.

Recent research indicates that a man officially turns into a grumpy old git at the age of fifty-two, but in truth it doesn't take much to set any man over the age of thirty-five off on a moan. A piece of chewing gum on a park bench, an extra two pence on the price of beer, a double-sheet toilet roll with perforations that don't line up – anything can tip him over the edge. And what might start off as a grumble about people who say they'll call you back in ten minutes but don't, can quickly develop into a full-blown rant about bad manners, the youth of today, the education system, the government, God and Piers Morgan.

In *The Grumpy Old Git's Guide to Life*, a grumpy old man shares his pet hates with the world at large and the things that conspire to irritate him on a daily basis

– including people who talk loudly into their mobile phones on trains, financial advisers, TV ads for insurance companies, ringpulls on tins of food, people who eat with their mouths open, flies, toilets you have to pay for, people who tell you to 'have a nice day', online mystery prizes, budget airline extra charges, pushy parents, banks that bombard you with offers of loans, dog poop, Twitter and God-botherers. And let's not get started on customer helpline staff who ask if there's anything else they can do for you when they haven't done the one thing you've asked them to do . . .

Chapter 1

ARE YOU A GRUMPY OLD GIT?

There are many telltale signs to look out for if you think you might have turned into a grumpy old git. Though, chances are, if you've been bought this book by a friend or partner you probably don't need to check . . .

- When you return home after work or a trip to the shops you've at least three gripes to share with your partner

- You never miss an opportunity to moan

- Tuts and heavy sighs punctuate your conversation with disturbing frequency

- You have your own mug at work

- You start to feel like every other human being was put on this planet to irritate you

- You realize you've not laughed or smiled in weeks

- Any moments of happiness you experience are brief and fleeting

- You slam the door in the faces of carol singers

- You feel nothing at sight of a newborn baby or puppy

- When the grandchildren come round you're more concerned with your clean carpets than how big they've grown

- You're spending increasing amounts of time in the shed

- You start sending your food back in restaurants

- You wash your car most days

- The only thing you do twice at night is go to the toilet

- Your body starts to carry excess weight – and not just the bags under your eyes

- You can spell

- You want to hibernate for the winter

- You become obsessed with Sudoku

- When you stoop to pick something up, you try and think of other things you can do while you're down there

- You have too much room in your house but not enough room in your medicine cabinet

- Your anecdotes get longer

- You find daytime television rewarding

- You dream about prunes

- You choose a car for how robust it is rather than for its 0–60

- You never leave home without an umbrella

- You start turning out the lights for economic rather than romantic reasons

- You start complaining about the youth of today

- You no longer buy green bananas . . . just in case

- You begin sentences with 'In our day . . . '

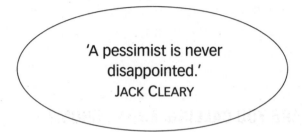

'A pessimist is never
disappointed.'
JACK CLEARY

Chapter 2

HOME DISCOMFORTS

WHO ARE YOU CALLING 'MATE', CHUM?

Have door-to-door salesmen ever stopped to think that the reason they are known as cold callers is because nobody ever lets them into the house? Indeed it is fair to say that in most homes these travelling chancers are about as welcome as dry rot or a visit from the bailiffs.

They tend to fall into two categories. The first glance up at your roof and tell you that unless all of your guttering is replaced immediately your entire house will fall down. They are easily recognizable by the fact that they could only look more like cowboys if they were wearing spurs and riding a horse. The second are desperate young company salesmen who are long on confidence but short on courtesy, and greet you as 'pal' or 'feller'. Feller? Do I look as if I chop trees? They go on to tell you that the new gas boiler – or whatever it is they are selling – will save you so much money that within two years it will pay for itself. So how does that work exactly? Has the boiler got a credit card?

The temptation is just to slam the door in their face, but occasionally you sympathize with their thankless task and try to let them down gently by saying: 'I'm sorry, this isn't really a convenient time.' So then they put you on the spot by asking when would be a convenient time. Now you have to come clean and explain that, as things stand, taking everything into consideration, you cannot envisage any time in the next thirty years when it would be convenient to talk to them. Then you slam the door in their face.

THE HILLS ARE ALIVE WITH THE SOUND OF DISTORTED BASS

You're sitting in your garden on a pleasant summer afternoon when the peace is disturbed by a fearful din coming from the house next door. Two weeks ago it sounded as if he was drilling for oil, last week his family appeared to be re-enacting the Battle of Britain in their back garden, now he is treating the entire neighbourhood to his CD collection. Why do people think their taste in music is so wonderful that it should be shared with everyone for miles around?

It's the same with the chavvy boy racers who roar through towns and cities in souped-up cars with the windows wound down. Buildings quake to the relentless thud, thud, thud, which is either the bass from their in-car stereo or the sound of their two brain cells banging into each other. You wouldn't mind if it was decent music, but it's never a nice bit of Motown or 'Bagpipes Play Hendrix'. That's one thing you have to say in favour of Simon Cowell: nobody ever turns up the volume on any of the songs for which he's been responsible.

COLD COMFORT

In bed, it's true what they say: one good turn gets most of the covers. You start off feeling snug and warm under the duvet, but in the middle of the night you wake up shivering with cold, feeling as if you've been put outside with the cat. It doesn't take long to work out why: your partner has dragged all the covers over to her side, leaving you suffering from exposure. When you try to reclaim the half of the duvet that is rightfully yours, you find that she has got it in the sort of vice-like grip normally reserved for a Scotsman and a fifty-pence piece. You have no option but to grin and bear it.

To add insult to injury, when she wakes up in the morning she says: 'Did you sleep well, darling? I did. This new duvet is lovely and warm.'

'Yes, well, I wouldn't know, would I?' you mutter darkly, while secretly planning to scupper a repeat performance by nailing the four corners of the duvet – and her, if necessary – to the wooden bed frame.

'Instead of getting married again,
I'm going to find a woman I don't like
and just give her a house.'
ROD STEWART

THERE'S A FLY! SEND IN THE SWAT TEAM

You're sitting at home relaxing in your favourite chair, reading the paper or watching the TV, when you first hear that ominous, distinctive buzzing sound. There's a fly in the room. If it would just mind its own business climbing the curtain or looking out of the window, you could happily ignore it, but instead it insists on whirring around your head, occasionally using your leg as a landing pad. You lash out wildly with the newspaper but the fly is always too quick for you, and that's what really grates – being repeatedly outsmarted by an insect.

You have a university degree, you hold a position of responsibility at work, you have raised two intelligent children (we'll forget about the third), you passed your driving test first time and you have a certificate for the 50 metres breaststroke; all a fly can do is, well, fly – and land on jam. Flies are even lower in the evolutionary chain than *Big Brother* contestants, and yet they are giving you the runaround. No wonder you hate them.

'God in his wisdom
made the fly
And then forgot to
tell us why.'
OGDEN NASH

STICK THIS . . .

Scotch tape – or sellotape – is one of those everyday commodities that it is difficult to imagine living without. It is useful for so many things – sticking your thumb to a parcel, sticking to itself so it turns into a huge gummy ball that won't get off your fingers . . . It can even give you an unexpected leg wax. The only problem is that after you have cut a piece off, the end of the tape is harder to find than the meaning of life. It blends in so effortlessly with the rest of the roll that the sharpest of fingernails or teeth struggle to locate it and prise it away – and if they do, the tape comes off in thin strips that are just about wide enough to bandage the legs of a Barbie doll.

Eventually, after much agonizing, you manage to peel off all the scraps and with subtle manoeuvring restore the tape to its full width . . . just as you reach the end of the bloody roll.

'My wife and I tried to breakfast together, but we had to stop or our marriage would have been wrecked.'
WINSTON CHURCHILL

THIS IS SUPPOSED TO BE A MOMENT OF WILD PASSION

You've both decided on an early night and things are just starting to get passionate when your partner suddenly leaps out of bed and announces: 'Sorry, I've just remembered something I need to add to tomorrow's shopping list.'

Aggrieved and deflated by the knowledge that she was clearly not concentrating on the matter in hand, you ask on her return to bed: 'What was so important that it couldn't wait?'

'Little cocktail sausages,' she replies. 'I don't know what made me think of them.'

THIS IS A STAIN ON MY REPUTATION

Most men hate decorating, if only because there are so many more pleasurable things you could be doing with your time than painting a white ceiling white again. It's such a tedious chore but, in your role as hunter-gatherer, you feel it is your duty to do it, and therefore you are determined to make a good job of it. Unfortunately fate often conspires against you.

It is almost inevitable that within three days of your having painted a room a small blemish will mysteriously appear on one of the walls. It may be a rogue splash of thick paint or a greasy mark, but one thing is certain: it will drive you to distraction. No matter where you stand in the room, your eyes are drawn to it as surely as if it were a photo of a naked Angelina Jolie. And each time you look at the mark, it seems to get bigger and more unsightly until, in your mind at least, it dominates the entire room.

Of course, your wife says it's nothing and tells you to ignore it, but you can't. Knowing there's still some emulsion left in the tin, you gently paint over the offending spot, but by now the rest of the wall has dried to a shade lighter with the result that your new artwork sticks out like a thumb that is not so much sore as positively throbbing.

There's only one thing for it: you head off to the DIY store and paint the whole room all over again. And yes, it's about as much fun as watching paint dry.

UM, THE CAT REALLY HAS GOT MY TONGUE

Let's get one thing straight: cats are fine, noble creatures. However they are also blessed with a personality which, if reproduced in humans, would see them locked away in a secure mental unit for a very long time as a danger to the public. You feed them, care for them, give them a home and how do they repay you? By sinking their claws, teeth or both into the most tender parts of your body while you're asleep. They're unpredictable to the point of being schizophrenic. One minute they're purring away happily on your lap, the next something has startled them and they're running off with a lump of your flesh in between their claws.

Cats also have a nasty habit of:

- coughing up a furball into your shoe

- breathing cat-food breath into your face last thing at night

- depositing dead mice in your bed

- inviting over all the other cats in the neighbourhood for a party while you're out

- attacking items of clothing while you're still wearing them

- refusing to get into their cat basket so that you can load them into the car to take them on 'holiday'

- getting pregnant at an obscenely young age despite all the talks you'd had about such matters

- running off with your socks

- driving away your car without permission – or maybe that was a dream.

No wonder cats are often associated with the devil.

'Cats are bastards . . .
If cats could find a way to push all
the people in the world into an active
volcano and still open all the tins
of cat food, they would.'
DAVID QUANTICK

WHO THE HELL'S AT THE DOOR?

When you are young your favourite times for sex are often first thing in the morning or last thing at night, but as you get older your body clock changes. You can't function in the morning until you have had breakfast and at night you are so tired at the end of a long day that you just want to go to sleep. On your agenda, sex comes somewhere below running a marathon or wrestling an alligator.

Therefore if you've got the house to yourselves, the ideal time for sex is during the day. By late morning your energy levels should be at their peak, so you switch on the telephone answering machine to ensure that you won't be disturbed and retire to bed. But then coitus is rudely interruptus by the ringing of the doorbell. Your immediate reaction is to ignore it, but then you think, 'What if it's that ornamental garden heron I ordered? If it goes back to the sorting office, I may never see it again.'

So you get dressed at breakneck speed and, after trying to put both feet in the same leg of your jeans and attempting to squeeze your head through the sleeve of your jumper, you stumble downstairs looking like someone whose natural habitat is a soup kitchen. The postman does not need to be Hercule Poirot to work out what you've been up to, but if there were any doubts they are quickly dispelled by the fact that you are wearing your underpants over your jeans. Unfortunately that is where any comparisons with Superman start and finish.

'This parcel's for next door,' says the postman cheerily, 'but there's nobody home, so can I ask you to take it in?'

Your jaw drops faster than your jeans did fifteen minutes earlier. The damned parcel isn't even for you! By the time you get back upstairs your ardour has softened. You can't even raise a smile.

'Shall I put the kettle on?' she asks.

'Might as well.'

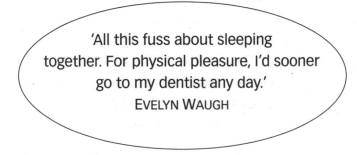

'All this fuss about sleeping together. For physical pleasure, I'd sooner go to my dentist any day.'
EVELYN WAUGH

NOT-SO-SPECIAL DELIVERY

Life is full of disappointments, like discovering that the expensive Labrador puppy you bought is really a hamster, finding that the last chocolate in the box is a coffee cream or the grim realization that you have reached the age where your knees buckle but your belt won't. Add to these the adrenalin rush of hearing the mail land with a veritable thud on your doormat. Aren't you Mr Popular today, you think? Well no, actually you're not, because out of ten items one is a bill and the other nine are all junk mail, offering conservatories you don't want to buy, pizzas you don't want to eat and promising special rates at a new nail bar which you have no intention of visiting, even if it does offer free biscuits on Wednesday afternoons. As you trudge back to whatever you were doing you take consolation from the fact that at least the bill is addressed to you personally.

'The music at a wedding procession always reminds me of the music of soldiers going into battle.'
HEINRICH HEINE

SLIMY LITTLE SO-AND-SOS

When it comes to considering the slimiest pests in the world today, we are spoilt for choice. Bankers, lawyers, estate agents and politicians can all present compelling claims to the crown, but for a gardener there is only one winner – snails. Together with their homeless chums, slugs, they wreak havoc in our borders, munching their way through our choicest plants. Slug pellets can be harmful to pets, so gardening experts suggest alternative ways of eliminating slugs and snails. The problem is none of them actually work. For example:

- Sprinkle a layer of grit or gravel around the plant. This is supposedly uncomfortable for slugs and snails to slither across, but the holes in the leaves the following morning suggest they're as happy on gravel as Torvill and Dean are on ice.

- Set down beer traps. Apparently slugs and snails are attracted to beer and will drown in it. But why should they die happy? Surely they don't deserve such a pleasant end? In any case, all their pals turn up to the party, which means that you end up with twice as many slugs in your garden as before. All in all, a waste of good beer.

- Encourage frogs, their natural predators. However, with over fifty slugs per square metre lurking beneath your flower beds, not even an amphibian Mr Creosote can eat them all.

- Put down ground coffee. Not only is this old remedy largely ineffective, the caffeine rush probably gives the slugs and snails more energy to carry on munching.

The only real solution is to catch the little buggers red-handed, at which point you can either slice them through with a trowel or pour salt onto them. This causes them to foam up like an ice cream soda before suffering what must be a horrible, slow and hopefully painful death. Even more marvellously, you can celebrate this merciless act of revenge by drinking all the beer you saved.

THAT'S A WHOLE DAY'S WORK I'VE LOST!

Power cuts really do make you grumpy, because they occur without warning. You're on the computer just in the middle of writing something when

HELLO, HELLO. IS ANYBODY THERE?

When you answer the phone and the line just goes dead without anyone speaking, your immediate fear is that you've got a crazed stalker. You never think it's one of those wretched companies that make computerized random calls to hundreds of households at a time but only follow up a handful – and whose executives should be subjected to a similar bombardment night after night, all through the night, for the next three months. Nor do you ever think it's a wrong number, made by somebody who is apparently too busy or too rude to go to the trouble of saying, 'Oh, I'm sorry I've got the wrong number,' before hanging up. No, you automatically assume a silent call is sinister, which is obviously completely irrational – unless you can hear heavy breathing or the postman happens to deliver a horse's head the following morning.

CAMERON, CAMERON, TAKE ME NOW!

You're lying on a sun-kissed beach sipping pina coladas next to Cameron Diaz. She's wearing a skimpy bikini and licking her lips in anticipation of returning to your hotel room for an afternoon of red-hot sex. You reach over and run your hands through her beautiful shiny hair when your wife barks: 'What do you think you're doing, you fat oaf? Take your hands off me! You've woken me up!'

It was all a dream, and you've been jolted back to reality with a vengeance. Instead of a revealing bikini and a sensuous smile, Cameron is now wearing an ankle-length winceyette nightdress (which could scarcely be less penetrable if it were fitted with padlocks) and a frosty expression. Instead of two hours of passion in a five-star beach hotel, you are faced with the prospect of getting ready for the arduous one-hour journey to the office through rush-hour traffic. The more you think of the glamorous lifestyle that has been snatched away from you in an instant, the grimmer the day ahead of you seems. And the worst thing is, it's not even started yet.

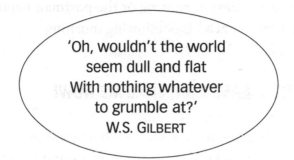

'Oh, wouldn't the world
seem dull and flat
With nothing whatever
to grumble at?'
W.S. GILBERT

MORE THINGS THAT MAKE US GRUMPY AROUND THE HOUSE

- finding someone else's pubic hairs in the bath – then running out of hot water

- discovering immediately post-poop that the toilet paper has run out and you are the only person in the house

- finding forks in the knife drawer

- people who squeeze the toothpaste from the top of the tube

- finding toenail clippings in the bed

- pens that mysteriously go missing from your desk

- stubbing your toe on the corner of the bed

- jars that require a vice to remove the lid

- finding a pile of crumbs in the butter container after the knife has been used to spread toast

- walking around in socks or bare feet and standing on an upturned electric plug

- paintbrushes that moult with each stroke, leaving stray hairs on your newly painted doors

- discovering that instead of recording the late-night football, the DVD player has recorded a Hungarian art-house animated film with subtitles

- other people's car alarms that go off in the middle of the night

- walls that crumble at the first sight of a rawlplug and screw

- getting a paper cut

- looking in the medicine cabinet and not realizing until it's too late that you've got the mouth ulcer treatment mixed up with the Anusol.

Chapter 3

THE GREAT SHOPPING EXPERIENCE

THERE'S A REASON IT'S ON SPECIAL OFFER

Over recent years, presumably in a desperate bid to beat the recession, certain stores have started launching heavy promotional offers on items that are invariably incongruous with the products they actually sell. Thus you get to the checkout having bought a diary, a pack of envelopes and a birthday card, and the salesgirl says: 'Would you like a cut-price bar of chocolate with that?'

'Er, no. Why would I want a bar of chocolate with a diary, a pack of envelopes and a birthday card?'

'Because it's on special offer.'

'So are half the things in this store, like that Paris Hilton calendar and that Jamie Oliver autobiography, but I don't want those either.'

'But it's nice chocolate.'

'From my many years on this planet, I'm quite aware of what chocolate tastes like, thank you, but I'm afraid that when I go out to buy envelopes I don't automatically think: "I must get a bar of chocolate with that – it will make licking the gum a much more pleasurable experience."'

'So you don't want any chocolate then?'

'No. And I'm sorry that your company has got a thousand crates of the stuff in storage at Heathrow, but it's really not my problem. Good day.'

'All I ask Is the chance to prove that money can't make me happy.'
SPIKE MILLIGAN

A MYSTERY PRIZE? NO THANKS, I'D RATHER NAIL MY HEAD TO A DOOR

Oh joy! An email sent by a company you've bought something from in the past says you have won a mystery prize. Apparently it could be one of four things: £1 million in cash, a brand new Mercedes car, two weeks in Barbados or a bottle opener. There are no prizes for guessing which one you'll be getting.

Seemingly oblivious to the fact that their cover has already been blown, they press on, telling you that the mystery prize is definitely yours and will be despatched with your next order. They even include a picture of a Mrs X of Doncaster who was evidently so ecstatic at receiving her prize that she appeared to be on the brink of orgasm. But do they really think you're going to place a new order of £15 just to win a piece of cheap tat worth £1.50? They must think you're a prize idiot! Quite simply, nothing should persuade you to accept these mystery prizes on the Internet. Beware of geeks bearing gifts.

IS THIS A SHIRT OR A PINCUSHION?

You buy a new shirt, and the first thing you want to do when you get home is try it on. This is easier said than done, because first you have to remove thirty-seven pins from various points around the shirt, two strips of clear plastic from under the collar, pieces of cardboard from the collar and the back, and sometimes even plastic clips on the cuffs. By the time you've done all this, the shirt has gone out of fashion. And there's always one pin that you miss, only realizing the oversight when it jabs into your ribs the first time you wear it.

HAVE YOU GOT FIVE ITEMS OR LESS IN YOUR BRAIN?

Express checkouts at the supermarket are irritating enough just for saying 'five items or less' when grammatically speaking it should be 'five items or fewer'. But what really gets your goat is when someone tries to go through with twenty items in their trolley. Is it that they can't read? Is it that they can't count? Or is it that they think the checkout girl is so stupid she'll think five packs of beer constitutes one item?

The thing is that most of us are so law-abiding we wouldn't dream of violating this rule. Even if we discovered at the checkout that we had six items in our cart, we'd either join one of the long regular queues, adding half an hour to our shop, or we'd meekly return one item to the shelves. We'd rather manage without toilet roll for a week than be humiliated at the checkout.

But are the rule-breakers ever punished? Of course not. If there were any justice in the world, they should be forced to buy their next whole week's worth of groceries using the self-scanning aisle. They won't be flouting the supermarket code again in a hurry after they've been told there's 'an unexpected item in the bagging area' forty-five times in succession.

GIVE ME A CHANCE – I'VE ONLY JUST WALKED IN

Why do some store assistants believe that the quickest way to make a sale is to go up to a customer as soon as he walks in and ask: 'Can I help you?'

Do they think you have a photographic memory that can take in every item on the racks in less than ten seconds? Or do they think you look like a shoplifter who will tuck half a dozen shirts under your jacket unless you are closely monitored throughout your visit?

Either way, the enquiry merely puts your back up. You reply that you're 'just looking' and beat a swift exit. Not only haven't you bought anything but you're unlikely ever to darken the doors of that store again. No sale and no return.

WHY DO I ALWAYS GET THE SUPERMARKET TROLLEY THAT WANTS TO MAKE A BID FOR FREEDOM?

It's one of the mysteries of modern life: we can put a man on the Moon, we can find cures for countless diseases, we can even make kangaroo-flavoured crisps, but we are seemingly incapable of designing a supermarket trolley that goes in a straight line. Some shopping carts won't even go forwards, they will only move sideways like crabs, all of which makes navigating your way safely along the aisles about as achievable as trying to break the world land speed record with the handbrake on. Frankly, it is easier to steer a bucking bronco than a supermarket trolley.

Consequently what should be a routine excursion around the store turns into a life-threatening dodgem ride, resulting in a trail of crumpled metal and scuffed ankles. By the time wounded shoppers have limped to the checkout the scene resembles something from *ER*.

And if you've ever wondered how so many trolleys come to finish up in rivers, it's not because shoppers have dumped them there deliberately. On the contrary, they have been trying to return the damn things to the designated bays, but the carts' natural steering has taken them at right angles out of the supermarket car park and straight down the riverbank.

'Forget about being world famous, it's hard enough just getting the automatic doors at the supermarket to acknowledge your existence.'
DOUGLAS COUPLAND

'Sirs, I have tested your machine.
It adds a new terror to life and makes
death a long-felt want.'
HERBERT BEERBOHM TREE,
REFERRING TO A GRAMOPHONE

YOU CAN SHOVE YOUR WARRANTY WHERE THE SUN DOESN'T SHINE

It's not easy to buy anything these days without the salesperson trying to sell you a warranty. But if you buy a decent dishwasher, camera or washing machine, you don't expect them to fall apart after two years, so why should you pay extra just in case they do? With the money sales staff make on these 'extras' it's no wonder they are eager to sell them, so how long before they start pushing warranties on non-mechanical goods?

'A pound of cheese? Would you like to take out a three-week warranty with that?'

'A packet of biscuits? Would you like to take out a warranty to guard against the top one being broken?'

'A bag of wine gums? Would you like to take out a warranty against there being no yellow ones?'

WHAT THEY REALLY MEAN

Salespeople will tell you anything to make a sale. In fact they'd sell their own grandmother to you if you also bought an extended warranty. Here's a brief guide to what salespeople say and what they really mean:

- 'I've been authorized to give you a hefty discount'
  – 'I've been authorized to make you think I'm giving you a hefty discount'

- 'You're lucky, this is the only one we've got left'
  – 'We've been trying to get rid of it for ages'

- 'I've got a sweater just like this at home'
  – 'It lines the dog's basket'

- 'It will ride up with wear'
  – 'The sleeves are too long'

- 'You'll find it will stretch after a wash'
  – 'The sleeves are too short'

- 'Don't worry about that little mark, you can hardly see it'
  – 'If your surname is Magoo'

- 'There's no catch'
  - 'You just haven't spotted it yet'

- 'All the instructions are in the manual'
  - 'I haven't a clue how it works'

- 'This phone is slightly cheaper because it's a second'
  - 'It's broken'

- 'You've got a real bargain there, sir'
  - 'There's one born every minute'

'The minute you leave your house in the morning you see something that makes you grumpy.'
ARTHUR SMITH

I'M SORRY MY EARS ARE BLEEDING ON YOUR STOCK

Why do some clothes shops turn the in-store music up to full blast so that you can hardly hear yourself think, let alone conduct a conversation with the sales assistant?

'How much is this shirt?'

'I can't see any dirt. What do you mean?'

'Green. Yes, I know it's green.'

'So you admit it's clean.'

'Get someone to turn the bloody volume down!'

Youngsters probably don't mind their ears being assaulted with the latest gangsta rap sounds but sometimes grown-ups have to shop in these stores too. If a middle-aged man goes in to buy a pair of trainers but has the unnerving sounds of a Los Angeles ghetto blaring out at him, the chances are he will beat a hasty exit before the *CSI* team turn up.

IF I WANT YOUR OPINION, I'LL ASK FOR IT

You can always tell which stores have recently sent their staff on customer training courses, because when you get to the checkout with the shirt or whatever it is that you've purchased, they try to engage with you by saying: 'That's a nice shirt.'

And you think to yourself: 'Well, yes, that's why I chose it. If I'd thought it was a lousy shirt, I'd have left it on the shelf. That tends to be how shopping works.'

What do they hope you're going to say by way of reply: 'Yes, it is a very nice shirt and I really ought to buy six more identical shirts right now because it is such a nice shirt'?

And do they stop at shirts? What do they say when all you've bought is three pairs of underpants? 'Ooooh, I bet you'll look good in those, sir! They'll really show off your contours!'

Frankly, the whole thing is one step away from sexual harassment.

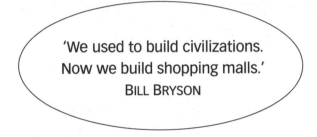

'We used to build civilizations.
Now we build shopping malls.'
BILL BRYSON

NO, I CAN'T EVEN SPARE A NANOSECOND FOR MARKET RESEARCH

It's impossible to venture into most towns these days without some woman with a clipboard approaching you and asking: 'Can you spare a minute for market research?' For a start, it's never a minute. The list of questions is so long that you're often in danger of hypothermia and missing the last nightbus home. And while the questions may seem innocent, you know that whatever answers you give will result in you being deluged with unwanted emails and cold calls for the next six months, trying to sell you everything from new double glazing to a funeral company loyalty card. In general, therefore, the safest course of action if you're approached in this way is to pretend that you're a member of a group of eco-warriors who refuse to engage in the capitalist culture by worshipping at the god of Mammon. Just make sure those half-dozen bulging shopping bags are well concealed behind your back before you attempt this.

Chapter 4

GRUMPY'S HALL OF SHAME: MUTTON DRESSED AS MUTTON

As you get older and grumpier it can be a thin line between looking cool for your age or looking like a total prat. Then there are those who don't even try. Some celebrities get things so wrong that even their stalkers won't be seen out with them and the only person that takes their calls is the plastic surgeon. It's 'stars' like this unsavoury bunch that really get grumpy's goat.

KEITH RICHARDS

Described by Elton John as looking like an arthritic monkey, Richards was still hooked on a diet of sex, drugs and rock 'n' roll at a time in life when he should have been at home enjoying a nice cup of tea and a biscuit.

BILLY CONNOLLY

The mane of hair was OK when he was young but now that he's in his seventies it just makes him look like one of those sad old guys you see on a park bench clutching a bottle of strong cider at nine o'clock in the morning.

CLIFF RICHARD

OK, how does he do it? He's in his late seventies and could still pass for fiftyish. Yes, the hair dye helps, and he readily admits to taking nine skin product tablets a day and moisturizing regularly, but there's got to be more to it than that. Nips? Tucks? He says not ... Maybe there is a portrait in the attic ...

'The best thing to do is to behave in a manner befitting one's age. If you are sixteen or under, try not to go bald.'
WOODY ALLEN

SIMON COWELL

So vain that he probably stalks himself, he has never met a mirror he didn't like but maybe he should take a closer look. The high-waisted trousers, tight black T-shirts, bouffant hair and sparkling white teeth all smack of a man desperately searching for the elixir of eternal youth but ending up with Lemsip. The result is that he looks more plastic than Barbie's boyfriend Ken – and considerably shorter. Sadly, as the music guru who brought the world Robson & Jerome, Teletubbies and Steve Brookstein, fashion is not even Cowell's greatest crime against humanity.

'A celebrity is any well-known TV or movie star who looks like he spends more than two hours working on his hair.'
STEVE MARTIN

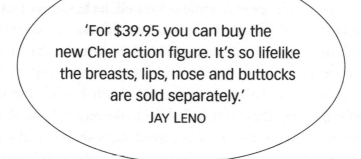

'For $39.95 you can buy the new Cher action figure. It's so lifelike the breasts, lips, nose and buttocks are sold separately.'
JAY LENO

DAVID GEST

With his permanently startled expression and a face that looked as if it had melted after being left too close to a fire, it is no wonder that Gest said he regrets ever having cosmetic surgery. 'I find it difficult to look at myself in the mirror,' he said, without a trace of concern for how the mirror must feel. He also revealed that his inspiration for having a facelift, a nose job and cheek implants was his friend Michael Jackson. A word of posthumous advice, David: when it comes to plastic surgery, perhaps Michael Jackson isn't the best role model.

ELTON JOHN

He could get away with fashion faux pas and crimes against good taste in his youth but there is surely no excuse for looking like a blancmange now he's in his seventies.

MICKEY ROURKE

Somehow it's even worse when a tough-guy actor resorts to cosmetic surgery. You couldn't imagine James Cagney having a nip and tuck or Champion the Wonder Horse having collagen implants.

Chapter 5

MONEY MATTERS

WHY IS IT CALLED A HELPLINE WHEN THEY NEVER HELP?

It's a known fact that insurance policies only cover you for things that are never likely to happen. You'll be handsomely protected in the event of being struck by a meteorite or attacked by a rampaging hippopotamus (providing you weren't away from home for longer than thirty days in any given six-month period) but try getting your money back if your garden fence blows down during a storm. No chance. So most of us never bother to claim – we just carry on paying the premiums year after year on the off-chance that we might bump into a hippo outside the library.

But occasionally you may think you have a valid claim and so you call the customer helpline. This is the point at which a young lady politely informs you that, no – surprise,

surprise – you are not covered, because section 48, clause 12f of your policy clearly states that in order to be covered for that particular eventuality you must be under sixty and a Scorpio. Then she says breezily: 'Is there anything else I can help you with today?' What does she mean, anything else? She hasn't helped you with the one thing you rang about. But do you tell her that? No, you thank her for her help and then grumble about it for the next hour to your long-suffering wife. It's what makes a marriage.

WHY ON EARTH WOULD I WANT ADVICE FROM YOU?

If for any reason you suddenly have a larger-than-usual amount of money in your current account – possibly because you are waiting to transfer it to a savings account elsewhere – you can guarantee that you will very quickly receive a 'courtesy call' from your bank. The money-grabbing antennae of someone in head office have tuned in to the fact that there's extra cash in your account and the bank wants to get its hands on it.

'So why are you calling?' you ask.

'It's just a courtesy call, sir.'

'You're not trying to sell me anything, I hope?'

'No, sir, just a courtesy call. I just wanted to say how

well you seem to be managing your finances, how nice your garden's been looking lately and how young you look for your age.'

'Uh, thank you. Well, if that's all, then goodb . . . '

'Actually, sir. There was one thing . . . '

'Oh, yes?'

'I notice that you have a little more money than usual in your account and wonder whether you would like to book an appointment with one of our financial advisers?'

'Correct me if I'm wrong, but your bank had to be rescued by the taxpayer three years ago after nearly going bankrupt whereas, by your own admission, I manage my finances quite well. So why would I want help from one of your advisers? If, however, you would like to book an appointment for me to give you financial advice, I'm free next Tuesday at eleven o'clock. My rates are reasonable.'

'A bank is a place that will lend you money if you can prove you don't need it.'
BOB HOPE

DO THEY NOT HAVE COMPUTERS IN BANKS?

Can anyone explain why a cheque paid into your bank account can take at least five days to clear? And these aren't just ordinary days, but working days. So weekends, bank holidays and afternoons when there's a big football match on the TV are not included.

You could walk from London to Paris in five days, you could fly around the world in that time and still have two days to spare, you could watch 240 episodes of *The Simpsons* in the same period, but banks apparently need longer than that to give your cheque the go-ahead.

They claim the delay is necessary to allow security checks, but in that time they could strip-search everyone you know. Of course it could be just an excuse to earn interest in transit on your money, but surely nobody would ever think banks could behave in an underhand, unscrupulous manner.

IF I WAIT HERE ANY LONGER, I'LL START GROWING MOSS

You decide to pop into the bank to pay in a cheque. 'You wait outside – I'll only be a minute,' you tell your partner with an optimism which proves that all your years on Earth have taught you nothing. Fifteen minutes later she peers through the window to see that you have moved forward approximately 9 inches – and that's only through fidgeting and a desire to kick the person in front – because you are stuck in a queue behind four people, including one who wants to open three different accounts for her grandson and another who has clearly never been in a bank before.

After much agonizing over whether to stay or not, you decide to see it through to the bitter end, knowing full well that were you to leave, the queue would mysteriously evaporate in an instant. Besides, there's no certainty that it would be quieter at any other time, particularly now that the branch only opens three days a week owing to 'restructuring' or, in plain English, 'cutbacks'. Finally you reach the front of the queue but just as you are about to step forward, the 'position closed' sign goes up at your window.

AAAAAAARRRRRRGH!

'What good is a long life to us if it is hard, joyless and so full of suffering that we can only welcome death as a deliverer?'
SIGMUND FREUD

'Dogs lead a nice life.
You never see a dog with
a wristwatch.'
GEORGE CARLIN

DOES 'VALUED CUSTOMER' JUST MEAN YOU THINK YOU CAN SCREW MORE MONEY OUT OF ME?

Why do banks only offer loans to people who don't want them? All your life you've struggled to make ends meet while raising a family and could really have done with a helping hand from the bank, but when you approached your friendly bank manager for a loan he made you feel about as welcome as a mouse head in a meat pie. Yet now that the kids have left home and you've finally got a bit of financial stability with some money in your account, your bank suddenly falls over itself to offer you money. Hardly a month goes by without a fresh offer of a loan or a platinum credit card at 'generous rates' (although it doesn't specify whether the rates are generous to you or to the bank) because you are apparently a 'valued customer'.

So were you a valued customer in 1985 when the bank manager laughed in your face when you asked him for a loan?

Or in 1989 when he said someone whose only security was Lucky Linda in the 2.30 at Belmont Park was a safer financial risk than you?

Or in 1994 when he threatened to bury your head in his pot plant if you didn't get out of his office?

No, of course you weren't. So he knows what he can do with his loan – and he can use his platinum card to pay for a proctologist to remove it.

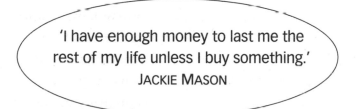

'I have enough money to last me the rest of my life unless I buy something.'
JACKIE MASON

I CAN'T REMEMBER MY MEMORABLE WORD

With the rise in instances of computer fraud, Internet security is clearly of paramount importance, which explains why it must be easier to break into Fort Knox than it is to access your online account. There are so many things to remember: your user-ID number, your password or security code number, your date of birth, plus your memorable word, which could be anything from your mother's maiden name or your first make of car to your favourite non-metallic element. And of course you're not allowed to write any of them down, which presents something of a problem when you've reached an age where you struggle to remember what day it is and the name of the woman you've lived with for the past forty years.

If you can't think of a memorable word, they will offer helpful suggestions such as the name of your favourite author or your favourite band. But these can change from year to year. You might have really liked Coldplay in 2009 but by 2010 you thought they'd gone off the boil and preferred Kings of Leon. What happens when your memorable word goes out of fashion?

'If you would know what the Lord God thinks of money, you only have to look at those to whom he gives it.'
MAURICE BARING

NO WIN, NO FEE – NO BRAIN

You can hardly move nowadays for companies offering to pursue your claim on a no-win, no-fee basis if you've suffered an accident at work that wasn't your fault.

- 'I leaned the ladder up against a jelly and was surprised when it collapsed.'

- 'My supervisor didn't warn me about diving in the vat of acid, so I assumed it would be okay.'

- 'Who would have thought that putting my hand in the moving blades to check they were still working could be dangerous?'

- 'I had often perched my lunchbox on a chainsaw. What could go wrong?'

- 'I balanced the ladder on a rocking chair. I was sure it would be safe.'

Don't these people realize that there is a reason why they suffered near-fatal injuries? It's called thinning the gene pool.

'Those who have some means
think that the most important thing in
the world is love. The poor know
that it is money.'
GERALD BRENAN

NEVER MIND ABOUT PEACE OF MIND, I'LL GIVE YOU A PIECE OF MY MIND

Insurance companies have clearly decided that anyone over the age of forty can be sent on a guilt trip. They calculate that as soon as we start a family we become concerned that when we die we will not be able to leave much to our 'loved ones'. Notwithstanding the fact that these are the very 'loved ones' who have bled us dry over the previous twenty years, the companies reckon that only by taking out a hugely expensive life insurance policy to cover our funeral costs will we be able to enjoy 'peace of mind' in our dotage. Otherwise apparently we will wake up screaming in the middle of the night that we're not going to be able to leave more than a measly few thousand to the wastrel son who once sold his sister to a weird religious cult so that he could use the money to buy a new pair of trainers. On the contrary, it's keeping up with the premium payments on the policy that will prevent us having 'peace of mind'.

To put across their message, insurance firms hire a respected senior celebrity, with a personal fortune that runs into seven figures, to tell us how much better we'll feel for signing up, and as an incentive for bankrupting ourselves we'll receive a free pen. Oh well, that's different! We'll do anything for a free pen. Here, take my house, take my wife!

Chapter 6

JOBS FOR THE (OLD) GITS

When it comes to the workplace, grumpy gits are all too often consigned to the scrapheap once we reach our fifties. What sort of mess would we be in if they had told Winston Churchill that at sixty-five he was too old to become prime minister in 1940 and that the job should go to a younger man, such as that chap from Germany with the funny moustache? Or if they had told Margaret Thatcher that at fifty she was too old to become leader of the Conservative Party and that the post should instead be occupied by a younger woman, such as Dusty Springfield? Or if they had told Ronald Reagan that at seventy he was too old and bewildered to become president of the United States? Actually, perhaps that's not such a good example.

Crustier workers still have much to offer. There are so many jobs to which they are ideally suited.

LITTER PICKING

Older people may not be the cause of most of the garbage that blights our streets but they are the perfect ones for collecting it, because with their natural stoop they are halfway to the ground anyway. Therefore they can do the job in half the time. Not only that but it's the perfect opportunity to curse the youth of today for dropping their sweet wrappers when there are perfectly good bins nearby.

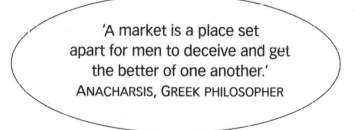

'A market is a place set apart for men to deceive and get the better of one another.'
ANACHARSIS, GREEK PHILOSOPHER

PIZZA DELIVERY

Isn't it annoying when you ring for a pizza and within five minutes it's at your door, before you've even had a chance to fetch the beers from the fridge or hunt for the remote? If restaurants used old git delivery riders, this wouldn't happen. Firstly they would insist on thoroughly polishing the bike before taking to the road, then they would tell any young people in the shop that flogging's too good for them and finally they would argue for fifteen minutes about which is the quickest way to the address. So instead of having your pizza delivered too quickly by a spotty youth whose complexion matches the margarita topping, how much better to have it brought to your door at a leisurely pace by a company where thin and crusty is a description of the delivery man.

TOILET ATTENDANT

Once you're more advanced in years, you never want to be too far from a toilet . . . just in case. Statistics reveal that senior citizens spend an average of 1 hour and 27 minutes each day either standing at or sitting on the lavatory. It's like a second home. So what better than a career that combines work with your hobby?

'One has to look out for engineers – they begin with sewing machines and end up with the atomic bomb.'
MARCEL PAGNOL

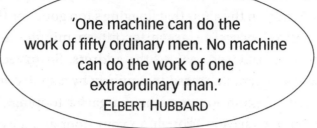

'One machine can do the work of fifty ordinary men. No machine can do the work of one extraordinary man.'
ELBERT HUBBARD

MARKET RESEARCH

Let's face it, there's nothing old gits enjoy more than a good snoop. Within five minutes of meeting a total stranger, they will know everything about him, including his wife's bra size, what his son does for a living and where he drinks. Give them a clipboard, and it's a licence to interrogate with a ferocity that the Spanish Inquisition would have baulked at.

DOCTOR'S RECEPTIONIST

This is the perfect opportunity for an old git to talk about other people's illnesses and operations all day long, and will take their mind off their own throbbing haemorrhoids. But because of the patient confidentiality ethic that governs the medical profession such information would be relayed only to their very closest mates in the pub.

POLITICIAN

It is an inescapable fact that our memory tends to deteriorate with age, but selective amnesia can prove a godsend when it comes to evading awkward political questions. What dodgy arms deal? What illegal cash donation? What blow job?

TAXI DRIVER

No group knows more about what is wrong with the world today than grumpy old gits. So place them at the wheel of a taxicab with a captive audience and they'll put the world to rights within minutes. A popular suggestion is that the restoration of capital punishment would resolve everything from the war in Iraq to Britney Spears's troubled love life.

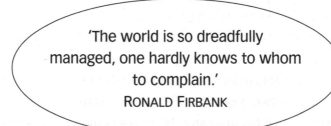

'The world is so dreadfully managed, one hardly knows to whom to complain.'
RONALD FIRBANK

Chapter 7

HEALTH CARE

HE'S SO FAT, EVEN HIS SHADOW HAS STRETCH MARKS

Don't you get sick of people moaning about how unhealthy they feel because they are overweight, when the only reason for their outsize girth is that they eat too much?

You've heard them: 'I can't play football with my grandson – it's my knees, you know.' And why are his knees in such bad shape? Because for the past forty years his legs have had to support a stomach the size of a small planet. It's like attaching flamingo legs to a rhinoceros. And it's all because his idea of a balanced diet is a bowl of chips in each hand.

Women are no better. 'I wonder why I can't fit into this dress from two years ago?' she will wail, searching for sympathy. Is it because she still labours under the delusion that drinking a Diet Coke alongside a cream cake cancels out its calories?

Instead of whingeing about their ballooning weight, these people should leave the gluttony to those who are pigs and proud of it.

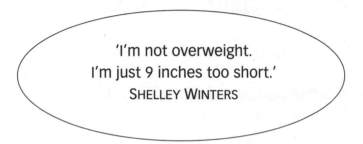

'I'm not overweight.
I'm just 9 inches too short.'
SHELLEY WINTERS

HICCUP HELL

You wouldn't think that something as simple as hiccups could prove so acutely embarrassing – yet the more you try to suppress them, the louder and more frequent they seem to become, creating a volume and force that could shatter glass or bring down a plane. Persistent hiccups will wreck whatever you are doing – whether it is eating a meal, watching a play in a theatre or having sex (not necessarily in the theatre).

Being slapped on the back, holding your breath and counting to fifty or drinking a glass of water are all supposed to cure hiccups, but no remedy works as well as a good shock. If your partner doesn't have a set of electrodes or a stun gun handy, the following remarks from her will almost certainly have a similar effect and cure your hiccups in an instant:

- 'I'm pregnant.'

- 'I've spent £1,500 on your credit card.'

- 'I've crashed your car.'

- 'The nanny is pregnant.'

PRAY, WHAT WAS THE POINT OF THIS APPOINTMENT?

Hospitals always impress upon you the perils of being late for an outpatient appointment. Punishment may range from a six-month wait for a new one to a visitation from a plague of locusts, depending on your postcode. So you do your utmost to arrive at the hospital at the stated time, only to find when you reach the waiting area that there are nineteen other people with 7.30 a.m. appointments. So how's that going to work with just two consultants? Are you going in ten at a time? Might it not be a little crowded in his room, not to say confusing with everyone shouting out their symptoms over the top of one another?

'Mrs Atkins, is it you with thrush? No? You're ringworm, okay. Well, I know one of you here has thrush, so come on, hands up, who is it?'

Mind you, that's not a consideration just yet, because there is no sign of either consultant. In fact they don't saunter in until eight o'clock – having no doubt enjoyed the hearty breakfast you didn't have time for – which means that it is 9.30 before you are eventually seen.

On your way out, you casually mention this to the receptionist and ask why you were given a 7.30 appointment when realistically there was never any prospect of your being seen until 9.30. She slowly puts down her Sudoku book, takes off her glasses and looks at you with that caring 'get out of my face, sick person' expression, which is your cue to thank her very much and leave.

IT MIGHT ONLY BE CRAMP BUT I'M STILL DYING

You know how it goes: you leap out of bed in the middle of the night in excruciating pain.

'What's the matter?' asks your partner, concerned.

'My leg, my leg!' you wail.

'What have you done?' she asks. 'Have you broken it? Have you strained it? Have you pulled a muscle?'

'No,' you reply breathlessly. 'It's cramp.'

'Oh, is that all?' she says, and turns over to go back to sleep.

That's the trouble with cramp – it's such a disappointing, unfashionable ailment. Real men break things, they dislocate things, they don't get cramp. You never heard of Evel Knievel being rushed off to hospital with cramp or Rocky pulling out of a big fight due to a nasty attack of cramp.

Cramp is so exasperating because you haven't really done anything to cause the undeniable pain. At worst you've allowed your legs or feet to get a bit cold, but that's no consolation as you hobble theatrically around the bedroom, yelling for a priest to read the Last Rites.

OUT, DAMNED SPOT

There are certain things you should have grown out of by the time you hit middle age – lying in bed all morning, wearing tight jeans, chasing sixteen-year-old girls. It's the same with spots. It's bad enough getting spots as a teenager but at least then you think that's your acne quota used up for life. So to get a new crop as an adult can make you particularly grumpy.

Since spots are par for the course for a teenager, nobody really comments on them, but if you get one or two in your forties people will say things like 'Ooooh, what's that on your face?' or 'That's a nasty spot you've got there.'

'Yes, thank you, I had noticed, but it is only a spot. However if I am growing a second nose – and you clearly think I am – then you have my full permission to pack me off to a freak show. I am most grateful for your concern.'

'It's been a rough day.
I got up this morning, put on a shirt and a button fell off. I picked up my briefcase and the handle came off. I'm afraid to go to the bathroom.'
RODNEY DANGERFIELD

BLESS ME, TRAINER, FOR I HAVE SINNED

Gyms are the new confessionals. In the same way that Catholics might repent their sins by going to Confession and saying three Hail Marys, the general belief is that if you lead a life of sloth and gluttony you can make everything right by going to the gym once a week.

To show their commitment to health and fitness, members drive to the gym in their car. Apart from a couple of minutes on a treadmill or lifting weights, they spend most of the next hour greeting friends in a way that says: 'Look at me, I've joined the gym, too. Do you like my training pants?'

Then they adjourn to the bar for a large glass of wine and a packet of crisps before driving home.

They could have expended more calories by staying at home and trying to open a jar of mayonnaise.

REALLY, YOUR BOWELS ARE NOT MY BUSINESS, THANK YOU

It's understandable that health-related matters become of more concern as you get older, but why do some people feel compelled to talk to complete strangers about their ailments and operations? It's as if a switch is activated in their brain on their fiftieth birthday dictating that future conversations should no longer be about football or fashion but about backache and varicose veins.

Doctors' waiting rooms are the worst places because the question 'What are you here for?' acquires the status of a chat-up line. And after forty minutes of listening to the woman next to you relaying her entire medical history, complete with photos, you feel like saying: 'Madam, it is not only your bowel that is irritable. I feel the same way – and if I have to listen to another minute of you going on about your various complaints, it won't be a doctor you'll need but an undertaker!'

'First the doctor told me the good news. I was going to have a disease named after me.'
STEVE MARTIN

Chapter 8

YOUR BACK GOES OUT MORE THAN YOU DO: HEALTH HINTS FOR GRUMPY OLD GITS

As you reach middle age there is an unfortunate tendency to pile on the pounds. You start watching your weight and before you know it everybody else is watching your weight too. You become so fat you need stabilizers. This only makes you feel grumpier. Whilst your attempts to keep in shape may ultimately only be successful if the shape in question is round, there are ways of giving both your body and mind at least a chance of staying healthy. If you can be arsed. Here are a few suggestions:

FROWN

It takes seventeen muscles to smile and forty-three to frown. So look miserable, it's good exercise for you.

DRINK PLENTY OF FLUIDS

Drinking a good amount of water is vital to your health. Dehydration can lead to fatigue, migraines, muscle cramps and constipation. Happily, a pint of beer contains mostly water and the repetitive action of lifting from bar to mouth, or indeed the energy required in propping up the bar, burns off plenty of calories.

CHEWING

British Prime Minister William Ewart Gladstone firmly believed that the key to a long, healthy life was to chew each mouthful of food exactly thirty-two times. Since he lived to the age of eighty-eight, perhaps he wasn't such an old duffer after all.

DIETING

Do the shelves in your pantry groan under the weight of bars of chocolate? Is your blood type listed as Ragù? Do you struggle to tell butter from middle-age spread? If so, you probably need to change your diet or, to put it scientifically, stop pigging out. Try saying no to third helpings of apple pie, or opting for the fruit creams rather than the truffle-based chocolates in the confectionery tin. Otherwise you might have to attend one of those classes whose names leave little to the imagination, such as Weight Watchers or Fat Bastards.

GARLIC

Garlic is highly recommended for keeping colds at bay, working on the simple principle of keeping at bay people who are likely to give you colds.

SLEEP

Studies show that sleep triggers changes in the brain that help improve memory. As good a reason as any for another afternoon nap.

LAUGHTER

If laughter really is the best medicine, why don't they have clowns instead of surgeons in hospital? 'TB? No problem. We'll just stick a custard pie in your face and squeeze a comedy car horn.'

SUDOKU

Crossword puzzles, word games and Sudoku all help to keep your mind active and alert. It is worth remembering, however, that they may have the opposite effect on your partner who has to put up with seeing you with your head buried in a puzzle book for hours on end.

SEX

During sexual intercourse the brain apparently undergoes seven chemical reactions which improve its functioning ability. For example, raised levels of oxytocin – the 'trust' hormone – increase a person's readiness to think of novel solutions to a problem. Shame that during sex your brain is rarely switched on, let alone functioning.

Chapter 9

GADGETS AND STUFF

MY PHONE IS MORE INTELLIGENT THAN ME

Whenever you go to buy a new mobile phone these days, it seems that you're not allowed to have one without a built-in camera. If you ask the shop assistant for a phone without a camera, it's as if you'd asked him to come up with an instant cure for cancer. Surely a phone is for making phone calls and a camera is for taking photos? There's a difference. Just as you wouldn't expect to get a decent tune out of a bucket or wash the car with a trombone, some of us don't expect – or particularly want – to be able to take photos with a phone. It's not as if the two things are interchangeable. Would Alexander Graham Bell have achieved such lasting fame had he tried to call Mr Watson in San Francisco on his new Kodak?

Of course, the salespeople tell you that camera phones can achieve the same quality as a professional photographer. This is true if the professional photographer in question has a bad case of the shakes and takes all his pictures through net curtains.

LEAVE ME ALONE, SEXY RUSSIAN GIRLS!

Obviously advertising is what makes the Internet world go round, but does it always have to be so 'in your face'? You can be visiting a perfectly innocuous website when suddenly an ad pops up before your eyes asking: DO YOU WANT TO DATE SEXY RUSSIAN GIRLS?

You say to yourself: 'No, actually, I just want to buy my wife a new bra. Is this a special offer where you buy an item and you get a free Russian girl? I suppose it could catch on as an alternative to air miles.'

And in case you still think sixties athletes Tamara and Irina Press are examples of sexy Russian girls, the ad helpfully shows a selection of scantily clad Eastern European beauties.

It's easy to say that all you have to do is close the ad and it will go away, but happily married men have been known to panic in such situations. One wrong click and a few days later they will have to explain to their wife why someone called Svetlana is waiting at the door wearing a fur hat, basque and suspenders.

'A world awash in information
is one in which information
has very little market value.'
PAUL KRUGMAN

DO YOU HAVE AN APP TO MAKE YOU SHUT UP?

Question: How do you know if someone has got an iPhone? Answer: They tell you.

Don't you get sick of iPhone bores? They say to you: 'My phone can tell me the current exchange rate on the Moldovan leu, what the weather is like in Buenos Aires and what time it is in Kuala Lumpur. What can your phone do?'

'It makes and receives calls. It's a phone. Now run along and see how the Moldovan leu is doing against the Mongolian scrote.'

MY PEN HATES ME

The phone rings and you quickly need to scribble down a number on a pad. You pick up the ballpoint pen that sits next to the phone and start writing. Nothing. Just a series of blank scrapes. What's it playing at? It was working perfectly an hour or so ago and you know it hasn't run out of ink. So you scribble away again – this time so aggressively that you tear a hole in the paper.

'I'm sorry,' you tell the person on the other end of the line, 'I can't get this pen to work.'

You shake it violently in the hope that you can knock some sense into it, you breathe warm air onto it in case it is cold, but still it refuses to produce anything resembling ink.

Hearing your distress, your partner brings you a replacement pen which thankfully works. After the call, you pick up the recalcitrant pen and, of course, it writes first time.

> 'If the human race wants to go to hell in a basket, technology can help it get there by jet.'
> CHARLES M. ALLEN

DOWEL M FOR MURDER

Flat-pack furniture was put on Earth to test man's patience. If he can assemble a bookcase using drawings that look as if they've been done by a two-year-old, with items that don't fit and with the obligatory missing part, then he should at least be capable of creating lasting peace in the Middle East.

According to recent figures released by the Royal Society for the Prevention of Accidents, 41 per cent of adults in the UK who have assembled flat-pack furniture admit to getting frustrated or angry by it, while 67 per cent have got into some form of 'difficulty'. Nearly 1 million people a year in the UK receive a minor injury while assembling flat-pack furniture, and of these injuries 50,000 are so serious that they need medical attention. And that's not counting the broken marriages.

Seeing the sturdy item in the showroom merely raises false hope, because when you open the box at home, all you find are a few pieces of wood. It scarcely looks any different from when it was on the tree. That is just the start of the disappointment as the whole tortuous process of building these cheap, cheerless contraptions is punctuated by the following phrases, usually accompanied by a sobbing sound:

- 'I'm sorry. It's not my fault. You'll just have to stand here holding it together when people come to visit.'

- 'This chair's got five legs. That can't be right. Can it? Can it?'

- 'What do you mean Bolt A8 has bolted? It's not funny.'

- 'Congratulations! We've got the world's first leaning CD tower!'

- 'Where's Dowel M? There's no Dowel M! If I can't find Dowel M, I'm going to kill someone!'

Of course some men will claim that self-assembly furniture is a piece of cake, and when you see their handiwork they'll tell you that they deliberately built it upside down to give it a distinctive look.

MY WAY OR THE HIGHWAY?

Sat Nav or GPS systems are useful tools for drivers, providing that the software and maps are right up to date. When you are solely relying on a gadget for directions, you don't want it sending you into a field of cows because it had failed to take into account the new motorway that had opened nearby eighteen months earlier.

The problem with these systems is that, unlike a human navigator, you can't have a frank exchange of views with them. If the GPS says 'Take a right turn in 50 yards' and you say 'Are you sure?' it either goes silent on you or it simply repeats its instructions, mantra-like. It's like sharing a car with a scientologist. And no one wants that.

> 'I can't swim.
> I can't drive, either.
> I was going to learn to drive but then
> I thought, well, what if I crash
> into a lake?'
> DYLAN MORAN

I RANG THE ENEMA HELPLINE – THEY WERE VERY RUDE

Is there a more misleading word in the English language than 'helpline'? Because almost without exception the staff are about as helpful as a poke in the eye with a sharp stick. They tell you nothing you want to know but merely suggest ways of upgrading – i.e. spending more money. That's if you can get through to them in the first place because of the 'high volume of calls we are currently experiencing'. And why are so many people calling them? Hmm, let's see. Maybe it's because their product is shite?

IT'S NOT JUST A TV REMOTE: IT'S A WINDOW INTO MY VERY SOUL

Women don't seem to understand the special relationship that exists between a man and the TV remote. Studies have suggested that the remote acquires such significance for men because it is an extension of our manhood. However, that can safely be dismissed as the usual academic nonsense until someone comes forward who is actually able to change channels by unzipping his pants.

The reason men are prepared to go to court over custody of the remote is that we feel we are the only ones to be trusted with making an informed decision on which sports channel to watch. If women were left in control of the remote, the family would be forced to suffer an endless diet of cookery programmes, costume dramas and films starring Leonardo DiCaprio. So that's why it's such a big deal for men when the remote mysteriously goes missing – and it's surprising how often such a substantial object does go missing. Of course we're not saying it's done deliberately, but if after the fifth remote of the year has gone AWOL and a random rummage in your partner's handbag (looking for a missing receipt, you understand) reveals five TV remotes lying hidden beneath a wad of tissues, it could be time to think about divorce.

ELECTRIC TOOTHBRUSH? I'VE ONLY GOT AN ACOUSTIC TOOTHBRUSH

In these days of health and safety, it's surprising that electric toothbrushes ever saw the light of day. You know the old adage about water and electricity not mixing? Well, just think of the amount of saliva that's in your mouth. It's a potential death trap.

What's the point of electric toothbrushes anyway? Are they designed for people for whom the act of gently moving one arm up and down for a couple of minutes twice a day is simply too strenuous? Let's face it, if you get exhausted just from brushing your teeth manually, dental care is the least of your worries. You should be investing in a pacemaker, not a toothbrush.

'One servant is worth a thousand gadgets.'
JOSEPH ALOIS SCHUMPETER

I'LL JUST PUT AN 'X' NEXT TIME

When a parcel is delivered to your door, the courier often asks you to sign for it. The old system involved the traditional, time-honoured and trusted method of putting your signature on paper, but with a nod to modern technology you are now asked to write it with a stylus pen on a small, touch-sensitive screen. Except that as soon as you make contact the pen slides around wildly all over the screen like a novice ice skater so that the end result resembles the work of a crazed spider. It certainly looks nothing like your signature and could never serve as proof of such, but when you mention this to the courier he simply shrugs and replies: 'That's all right, mate. They never do.' Which rather begs the question: what's the point of it at all then?

'Some mornings, it's just not worth chewing through the leather straps.'
EMO PHILIPS

'To err is human,
but to really foul things up
requires a computer.'
PHILIP HOWARD

OH MY GOD, I THINK I'VE JUST ACCIDENTALLY ADOPTED AN AFRICAN ORPHAN

Why must Internet websites use invasive advertising pop-ups that deliberately hide their 'Close' button? You hunt around for it with your mouse but it proves so difficult to locate that it would be quicker to get rid of death-watch beetle. So you start clicking away frantically all over the pop-up but instead of closing, it takes you to another screen where it appears that you are on the brink of buying something you don't want. One false click now and you could end up with a timeshare apartment in Spain or a Thai ladyboy. At times like this it's probably best to close the whole thing down and hope they've gone by the morning.

IS 'HELL' A EUPHEMISM FOR BEING KEPT ON HOLD?

What are the most terrifying five words you can hear in the English language?

- 'Mother's coming to stay tomorrow.'

- 'Next door's lion has escaped.'

- 'It's the taxman for you.'

They're all pretty scary, but none of these phrases can make your heart sink as quickly as: 'I'm putting you on hold.'

The trouble is they never tell you how long they're putting you on hold for. A minute or two is fine but it wouldn't surprise me if people had died of starvation while being kept on hold. Six months after death, paramedics would find a skeleton still clutching the phone and a voice at the other end saying: 'Thank you for holding. An adviser will be with you shortly.'

It's the same when they say 'your call is in a queue'. Well, how long's the bloody queue? Give us a clue, and then we'll know whether or not it's worth waiting.

In the meantime we're supposed to be satisfied with listening to some canned music. Since when have a few tinny bars of James Last been considered adequate compensation for one of life's disappointments?

- 'I'm sorry Paula's dumped you at the altar. Why don't you listen to some Peruvian pan pipes?'

- 'I'm very sorry I threw away the £90 million winning lottery ticket, but I've bought you a nice eighties medley CD to make up for it.'

- 'It's really sad about all eight members of your family being killed in that car crash. Hey, have you heard the latest Leona Lewis album?'

Chapter 10

HOLIDAYS AND LEISURE TIME

SO WHICH WILL IT BE? SUNBURN OR FROSTBITE?

Along with checking that your one pair of swimming trunks hasn't disintegrated in the drawer since you wore them last year and that your Hawaiian shirt won't frighten the horses, a ritual before going away on holiday is to check the online weather forecast for your destination so that you can decide what other clothes to take. You might as well ask an old woman selling sprigs of lucky heather or consult a psychic octopus, as forecasts for weather over three days away change completely every time you look at them.

Here are some better ways of predicting the weather:

- If cows are sitting in a field, it is going to rain.

- If cows are standing in a field, it is because the grass is too wet because it has been raining.

- If cows are sitting in a field with their umbrellas up, it is raining.

THIS ISN'T A SHOWER, IT'S AN INSTRUMENT OF TORTURE

One of the best things about staying in a hotel is the opportunity to have a long relaxing shower without having to worry about how much water you're using or whether your teenage daughter will start banging on the door at any minute screaming: 'Haven't you finished yet?' Depending on whether you've been lazing on the beach all day or hillwalking, you probably want either a cool or a warm shower, only to discover that it operates at just two temperatures – ice cold and scalding hot. Furthermore, these are separated by a turn of 0.009 mm on the dial. So one moment you are shivering like Scott of the Antarctic, the next clouds of hot steam are rising from your body as if you are about to erupt. You'd be a more comfortable temperature if you caught swine flu.

'Boy, those French: they have a different word for everything!'
STEVE MARTIN

UNFORTUNATELY I FORGOT TO PACK MY X-RAY SPECS

A familiar optional extra when booking a holiday is to pay a supplement for a room with a sea view. These add-ons don't come cheap, but the thought of gazing out from your balcony over an idyllic scene of boats drifting on a clear blue ocean makes you temporarily forget how miserly you are by nature. So it's something of a disappointment when you step out onto the balcony and are faced with nothing more picturesque than the walls of two hotels. Where's the sea view you've paid for?

In high dudgeon you phone reception to complain. A mere forty-five minutes later, a member of staff arrives at your room to see what the problem is.

'We've paid extra for a sea view,' you explain, 'but there isn't one.'

'Señor,' he says, leading you onto the balcony, 'you see there is a small gap between the two hotels in front of you?'

'Yes.'

And if you look along that gap, you see something blue at the end, yes?'

'Yes.'

'That's the sea.'

'But I can only see about an inch of it.'

'It's the sea.'

'But it's not what I call a sea view.'

'It's the sea. You can see it, so it's a sea view.'

'But it's hidden by those hotels.'

'What do you want me to do?' he shrugs. 'Knock down the hotels? Move the sea?'

And with that he departs.

For your information, my Spanish friend, the following do not constitute a sea view:

- if you have to use a telescope

- if you can only see the water by hanging right over the balcony and twisting your head at an angle of 90 degrees while your partner holds on to your ankles

- a mural of the sea.

'The world is so dreadfully managed, one hardly knows to whom to complain.'
RONALD FIRBANK

JUST WHAT I WANTED TO HEAR – SLOVAKIAN KARAOKE

Holidaying in a smart Mediterranean resort hotel has many plus points. The hotel entertainment is rarely one of them.

The acts mainly consist of a busload of Eastern European boy/girl duos who tour the hotels in the area performing the same cheesy songs. They dress as if they were still in the 1970s and usually have single-word names, like Harmony, Moonbeam or Crap. He stands at the keyboard, which – like his English – sounds broken, while she dances around with moves that are intended to look sexy but suggest instead that she is in urgent need of the toilet.

On other nights you will be treated to 'cabaret' (some guy who juggles clubs or does strange things with hoops), a magician who can make doves fly but not time, and an 'international singing artiste' – a woman of a certain age from Wigan who says things like, 'This song has been very good to me,' before failing to return the compliment.

For a more enjoyable evening, you would be better off taking a refreshing stroll along the seafront whilst having all your valuables pickpocketed by the smiling locals.

THAT'S MY SUNLOUNGER AND I HAVE THE PAPERWORK TO PROVE IT

It's a sad fact that when on holiday you often take more care of your sunlounger than you do of your passport. Quite why you become so possessive about a cheap piece of white plastic that you have never met before and will have but a passing acquaintance with anyway is something of a mystery, but once you have laid claim to it you have absolutely no intention of letting it go. If you have to leave it for more than a minute you drape it in a towel and, particularly if it's a standard hotel towel, you add that personal touch with the paperback book of your choice. The presence of a Len Deighton thriller on top of the towel sends out an unmistakable warning message to every other guest at the hotel. Short of attaching a Doberman to it, there's not much more you can do.

If, however, strong winds should dislodge your markers and you return after lunch to find another couple occupying your sunloungers, the ensuing debate is like a re-enactment of El Alamein. In the aftermath, it is not unusual to see grown men raging and weeping at the injustice of life as if they had lost their own child.

The following day, unless you get up in the middle of the night to reserve your place around the pool by torchlight, the chances are you will be lying on a different sunlounger.

Nevertheless you will now defend your new plastic chair as fiercely as if it was a priceless family heirloom.

WHY DO I NEED A DEGREE IN PLUMBING TO TURN ON A TAP?

Operating a tap was always a task within the capabilities of even the most committed technophobe. You simply turned it and water came out. It was a principle that served the world nobly for centuries. But now when you go into a public washroom or a hotel, you never know what sort of tap you're going to be dealing with. Is it a traditional one that you turn; is it one you have to push down forcibly, sending a jet of water everywhere except on your hands; is it one that is worked by foot; is it one with a handle that lifts up; is it one with a handle that moves sideways; or is it one where you wave your hands under the tap for five minutes, eventually prompting a meagre sprinkle of water to descend?

Since there is rarely a clue as to what type of tap it is, customers have to resort to trial and error. You have to virtually dismantle some taps before they will yield the secret of their operation. Presumably the idea of these fancy new devices is to conserve water, but as you get so confused that most of it floods the floor and the front of your trousers, it rather defeats the object.

PUTTING THE 'W' IN ANCHORS

If you're staying in a hotel in mainland Europe, the chances are that the TV in your room will only have a couple of English-speaking channels, one of which is usually CNN. Whilst its news coverage is certainly comprehensive, you find yourself paying scant attention to the world's events because you are distracted by the presenters' habit of emphasizing EVERY other WORD. By way of a change, sometimes they simply choose to emphasize the wrong words, as in: 'Dozens OF people in the NEIGHBOURHOOD fled today AFTER a house fire broke OUT in Louisville, Kentucky.'

There is no such thing as a quiet news day on CNN as the overexcited anchors strive to inject drama into the most mundane story. They could make a church fete sound like an international crisis. After five minutes of these vocal gymnastics you can stand no more. Now what channel was that Albanian game show on?

GOLF: GETTING BEATEN BY CLUBS

When Mark Twain described golf as 'a good walk spoiled', he knew a thing or two. Any golfer who, in the course of a round, has spent almost as long in a bunker as Hitler will testify that it is the most frustrating of games and one which, no matter how badly you play, it is always possible to get worse. Here are just some of the things that drive golfers not only to distraction but sometimes out of bounds:

- hitting a tree and being further away than when you started

- hitting a perfect draw or fade but not knowing how you did it

- people who spend an eternity lining up their putt just because the professionals do it on TV

- a stream emerging from nowhere to swallow your ball

- people who cough halfway through your backswing

- after putting all your strength into a tee shot you peer into the distance, only to find that the ball is resting next to your foot

- know-alls who, without you asking, tell you what's wrong with your swing

- when your drive hits your playing partner flush in the head so that you end up making a double-bogey and having to buy a wreath.

'There is a very fine line between "hobby" and "mental illness".'
DAVE BARRY

I DIDN'T KNOW THEY HAD NOVELTY KEYRINGS IN MEDIEVAL TIMES

Have you noticed that when they built stately homes and castles hundreds of years ago they always put the gift shop on the way out? Was this so that after raping the womenfolk and pillaging their possessions, the invaders would at least have to stop and buy a souvenir mug or a furry-topped pencil before making their escape?

'He who laughs has not yet heard the bad news.'
BERTOLT BRECHT

'I didn't like the play, but then I
saw it under adverse conditions –
the curtain was up.'
GROUCHO MARX

CURB YOUR ENTHUSIASM, PLEASE

When you're at a concert, why do people burst into
spontaneous applause – and sometimes a standing ovation
– as soon as they hear the first few bars of a familiar song?
Wait until you know whether he's going to perform it
properly first. He might be really awful tonight, hopelessly
off-key, but you've already wildly applauded him, in which
case what are you going to do when he finally struggles
tunelessly to the end? Sit in stony silence? Boo him?

It's the same with those old American TV comedy
shows. The moment the star or any popular character
walks on stage, the audience starts clapping, whooping
and hollering like it's the Second Coming. Why? Lucille
Ball hasn't even done anything funny yet. All she's done
is walk a few yards without falling over the set. She hasn't
even screeched. Save your applause until it's been earned.

Even crazier are people who applaud at the end of a

movie. It's like talking to the television set. They can't hear you, you know!

THIS PLAY STINKS

Theatre billboards traditionally promote their shows with review notices promising 'an evening of jolly good fun' or 'absolutely hilarious'. But in these competitive times some theatres try to outdo the opposition by using phrases like 'pantswettingly funny'. Might this not be counter-productive? Would you really want to sit in a warm theatre for two and a half hours next to someone who has just lost control of his bladder?

'I go to the theatre to be entertained.
I don't want to see rape, sodomy,
incest and drug addiction.
I can get all of that at home.'
PETER COOK

Chapter 11

THINGS THAT WERE BETTER IN OUR DAY

Everyone knows that things were better in our day. Sure there were wars, riots and assassinations, our diets were terrible and we smoked like chimneys but on the other hand nobody then had even heard of Jessica and Ashlee Simpson.

THE WEATHER

Never mind all this global warming stuff with polar bears having to move into Hillary Clinton's bed to find somewhere cold – it was always sunnier and hotter when we were young. The skies were perpetually blue and we didn't have to venture out in the height of summer under four layers of clothing and a balaclava in order to protect ourselves from the sun's harmful rays. In those days the sun was our friend. Now it is the devil incarnate, going from hero to zero almost as fast as Marion Jones.

HOUSEHOLD APPLIANCES

There was a time when television sets, vacuum cleaners and washing machines all used to last for years while a refrigerator received as a wedding present could very nearly outlive you. Nowadays these items contain so many cheaply made parts that they break down as soon as they are out of the packaging. Indeed the bubble wrap is often the sturdiest part. Consequently the mayfly has a longer life than the average household appliance.

'Inanimate objects are classified scientifically into three major categories – those that work, those that break down and those that get lost.'
RUSSELL BAKER

'What we call "progress"
is the exchange of one nuisance
for another nuisance.'
HAVELOCK ELLIS

PAUL McCARTNEY

Once upon a time he was the fresh-faced composer of some of the greatest songs in the history of popular music. But then he began to decompose. It all started with 'Mull of Kintyre' and went steadily downhill after that. He still keeps churning out albums but why does he bother? I think we'd all be happy if he just went away quietly and ran a health farm.

MANNERS

The time was when even total strangers would say 'good morning' to each other if out for a walk but nowadays you just get a blank look or some knuckle-dragger snarling,

'What are you looking at?' 'Well actually I'm looking at how in your case evolution appears to have gone in reverse.' And it's not only teenagers – the twenty-somethings are just as bad. Not that they ever walk much anyway – they would rather drive their gas guzzlers 20 yards than make the same journey on foot. Meanwhile little old ladies are only helped across the road so that they can be relieved of their purses and there's more chance of a dodo being seen strolling down Oxford Street with a Selfridges bag under its wing than of someone on a bus or train getting up to offer you their seat.

ART GARFUNKEL'S HAIR

The Lord giveth Art Garfunkel the voice of an angel but in return he taketh away his hair. Even in his prime Art had something of a high forehead but his mass of curls gave him a certain boyish charm. The perm is still there but it has retreated so far on to the top of his head that it is in danger of sliding down the back. He resembles a crowned crane in courtship mode. Today's style may look like a topiary but sadly it is no great work of Art.

SHOES

Back in the day you could trust your shoes like you trusted your bank manager. Both were solid, reliable and protected you from an uncertain climate. Nowadays you wouldn't trust your shoes any more than you would trust your bank manager. Both are smooth, slippery, lack substance and sole, fall apart in a crisis and can leave you seriously out of pocket. Decades past may have offered a limited choice of style and colour but at least these shoes looked as if they had been assembled with something stronger than Blu-Tack. Today you pay an exorbitant price for a pair (and that's not including the special spray, buffer and toner), wear them once in the rain and they leak. And when you return them to the store, the sales assistant tells you that it's your fault – you shouldn't have worn them outdoors! Also they never have any shoes in your size. If you're a UK size 11, what is the point in the sales assistant telling you, 'We've got them in a 9?' 'Right, thanks. If I lose all my toes to frostbite, I'll be sure to come back.'

TELEVISION

There may be dozens more channels now, but TV was indubitably better in our day. *The Lone Ranger, Batman,*

The Avengers, *Deputy Dawg* – all classics of their genre, and not a makeover or so-called reality show in sight. And the only F word was Flipper. To illustrate how far standards have fallen, Jethro from *The Beverly Hillbillies* would be reading the news today.

'I have had my aerials removed – it's the moral equivalent of a prostate operation.'
MALCOLM MUGGERIDGE

DOCTORS

They used to make house calls to visit sick patients but now if you have the use of one leg, your temperature is below 109 Fahrenheit and no body parts have actually fallen off, they say you are well enough to get to the doctors' surgery . . . unless they have a golf game arranged for that day.

U2

Back in the 1980s, U2 were a great band, creating classics such as 'New Year's Day' and 'The Unforgettable Fire'. Now all Bono appears worried about is saving mankind and qualifying for sainthood. Make Bono history.

CHILDREN

We were well-behaved children, except when it came to eating our greens, doing physics homework instead of watching Huckleberry Hound or kissing elderly aunts with moustaches. The worst thing we ever did was pull a girl's pigtails and the most dangerous item we ever took to school was meant to be spaghetti bolognese for a domestic science lesson. The nearest we came to a gang was joining the after-school chess club. But so many kids today are almost feral. They have no respect for authority, they are completely out of control and their vocabulary is appalling. Most of them think a thesaurus was a creature from *Jurassic Park*. I blame the parents. No, wait, that's us.

CHARLES, PRINCE OF WALES

In his younger days he was merely out-of-touch and old-fashioned, as comfortable in social gatherings as Mr Bean. Men took comfort from the fact that as long as Charles was around, they could never be accused of being the world's worst dancer. He was seen as a harmless eccentric who talked to his plants because it was much like talking to his family. Then we learned that his old-fashioned approach extended to the time-honoured royal tradition of taking a mistress. Henry VIII would have been proud of him. Unlike Henry, Charles has yet to have any of his wives beheaded although in Camilla's case such an act would surely qualify as beauty therapy.

THE ABILITY TO COPE

We prided ourselves on being able to cope. We coped with the Second World War, we coped with rationing, we coped with Spam, we even coped with Glam Rock. We dealt with crises on an almost daily basis but never complained or wallowed in self-pity. The amputation of a leg often warranted nothing more than a quick trip to outpatients and later that day we were hopping around as if nothing had happened. But nowadays people are forever claiming that they are too stressed to cope and turn to counselling for help with everything from a broken fingernail to a blocked drain. If your house catches fire, your first call really should be to the emergency services not your therapist. In America therapists have their own therapists while for many celebrities a spell in rehab is as important on their CV as their own TV special. Clinics like The Priory in London resemble showbiz auditions. Get a grip!

SWEETS

Remember when you could go into a sweet shop and choose from a wonderful selection of jars lining the shelves, containing such myriad candy delights as Tom Thumb drops and pineapple chunks or scour dozens of boxes lined up along the counter for Black Jacks or jamboree bags? Well, no more. Such establishments are now a seriously endangered species; all you can buy in most sweet shops are chocolate bars so expensive that the only thing which melts in your hand is your money.

SANTA'S 'ASSISTANTS'

We all know that the real Santa Claus is a busy man and so he needs plenty of lookalikes to help out in stores across the world at Christmas time, but sadly standards have been allowed to slip. Go into any store's Christmas grotto twenty-five years ago and Santa was always played by someone who looked the part. He may not necessarily have been jolly (understandably after being climbed on and having his false beard tugged all day), some of his ample girth may have been padding and the cause of his rosy cheeks could usually be smelt on his breath, but at least he measured up. By comparison today's Santas appear positively anorexic, as if the last good meal they had was the previous year's mince pie left at the bottom of the chimney. The costume hangs on them so limply they look more like red vultures. Niles Crane would make a more suitable Santa than most of them. And they finish it off by wearing training shoes on their feet! Has nobody ever told them that you need sturdy boots for ploughing through snow, not footwear that is one step up from ballet pumps? What would have happened to Captain Scott if he had gone to the South Pole wearing trainers? He'd have caught his death . . . Well anyway, it's not right.

GEORGE MELLY:
How come you've got more lines on your face than me?
MICK JAGGER:
They're laughter lines.
GEORGE MELLY:
Surely nothing's that funny.

Chapter 12

TRAVEL AND TRANSPORT

BUT WHY CAN'T YOU PUT CHILDREN IN THE LUGGAGE HOLD?

If parents must take their children on holiday with them because all the kennels are fully booked, there should be a law against any under the age of ten travelling on planes. There are two types of children on planes; there's the fractious baby who cries throughout the flight – and that's even before he's tasted the in-flight meal – and there's the child behind you who passes the time by repeatedly kicking the back of your seat. Why does he do this? Is your seat the only one on the plane with a target painted on the back? Or is he trying to simulate turbulence? By the time you land your back is so bruised it looks like you had taken on a kangaroo at taekwondo.

EXACTLY WHAT KIND OF 'BUDGET' IS THIS AIRLINE CATERING FOR?

Want to know how to turn £5 into £100 in just two minutes? Try booking a flight with a budget airline. You start off with what appears a nice cheap flight but by the time you've added on all the various extras such as fuel charges (yes, it would be good if the plane had some fuel), airport tax, airport check-in fee, baggage fee, pre-allocated seat fee, fast-track security lane fee, priority boarding fee, in-flight meal fee, additional leg room fee, online booking fee, and credit or debit card fee, the price has taken off faster than the plane itself. It would be cheaper to fly to the Moon.

In view of the fact that serious consideration has been given to charging for using the in-flight toilet, it's surprising that airlines haven't yet introduced any of the following:

- demonstration charge – for £100 trained pole dancers will perform the safety demonstration routine

- pilot charge – for £200 (£500 for take-off and landing) a passenger gets to fly the plane for a couple of minutes

- mile-high club charge – for a bargain £30 you can buy a condom and a plastic red rose to take in to the airplane toilet with your partner or whoever takes your fancy on the flight

- parachute charge – for an extra £150 you can have a parachute under your seat as well as a flotation device, to cover all eventualities

- delay charge – a £50 fee which is refundable if your flight is delayed by more than six months.

'If God had intended us to fly, He wouldn't have invented Spanish air traffic control.'
CRAIG CHARLES

IT'S BEEN SO LONG SINCE I SAW MY LUGGAGE I CAN'T REMEMBER WHAT IT LOOKS LIKE

The first law of air travel states that if you're in a hurry to get away from an airport to catch a train or a bus, your luggage will be last off the carousel. Unclaimed bags can do eight or nine laps before your suitcase finally limps into view, battered, misshapen and almost unrecognizable from the last time you saw it, courtesy of the tender, loving care of the baggage handlers. You can try anything: checking in early, checking in last, buying a fluorescent pink suitcase, painting a smiley face on it, sticking go faster stripes on it, but nothing works. Your bag is simply destined to be last.

WHAT MAKES YOU THINK I CARE WHETHER SAMANTHA IS SEEING MICHAEL FROM ACCOUNTS?

A slogan much loved by rail companies for many years has been: 'Let the train take the strain.' Fat chance! Not by the time you've found that there's nowhere to put your luggage, that an 18-stone Bulgarian weightlifter is sitting in your reserved seat and there's no buffet service to deliver you a selection of overpriced snacks. And that's before all the mobile phones come out to play.

Why do people on trains feel the need to talk loudly and almost endlessly into their phones? As soon as they finish one call, they start on another, wittering on about everything from cousin June's blonde highlights to the latest workplace gossip. Did you know that Clive in Showers and Fittings is on report for gross misuse of a cubicle and that Joan in Knobs and Knockers has been spotted coming out of a hotel with Maurice from Goods Inwards? Do they think the other passengers really give a damn? Yet as a captive audience we are forced to listen to every word, unless we counter with our own social menace, the iPod at full volume.

Then there are the thrusting business types who try to prove how indispensable they are by remaining in constant contact with the office because obviously it couldn't possibly function without them for half a day. And of course they insist on doing this at the top of their voices because the first rule of mobile phone law states that the volume with which an individual speaks into the phone is in inverse proportion to that individual's personal importance. With any luck, just as they are in full flow, the train will enter a tunnel where reception is non-existent, leaving them cursing privately while you savour every one of its 2,358 yards in peace.

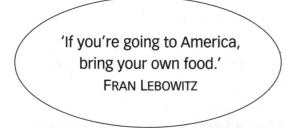

'If you're going to America, bring your own food.'
FRAN LEBOWITZ

'Of course, America had
often been discovered before Columbus,
but it had always been hushed up.'
OSCAR WILDE

STOOL PIGEONS

Why is it that as soon as you've washed your car, some pigeon that has spent the afternoon watching Spitfires in old war movies passes overhead and craps all over it? Sometimes there's so much mess it's like giving the car a white paint spray job. What do these birds eat all day – prunes and All-Bran?

WHY CAN'T THEY ALL SPEAK ENGLISH?

A recent survey conducted by a travel company revealed some of the embarrassing mistakes made by Britons attempting to speak a foreign language while abroad. They included:

- calling a Greek a 'squid' in the morning, because

'kalimera', the Greek for 'good morning', sounds remarkably similar to 'calimari'

- making a Frenchman choke over his dinner by mispronouncing 'je suis plein' ('I am full') as 'je suis pleine' ('I am pregnant')

- asking a Portuguese person for something rather intimate at the breakfast table, because 'preservativo' does not mean 'jam' in Portuguese but 'condom'.

Of course none of this would happen if everyone in the world did the sensible thing and spoke English.

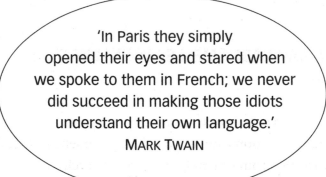

'In Paris they simply opened their eyes and stared when we spoke to them in French; we never did succeed in making those idiots understand their own language.'
MARK TWAIN

I DON'T CARE IF IT'S FOR CHARITY – JUST GET OUT OF MY WAY

It's so frustrating when your travel plans are thrown into confusion because busy roads are closed to traffic for a city marathon. Why can't they just run around a field hundreds of times instead? Or if they're that fit surely they could dodge out of the way of approaching buses, cars and trucks? Some authorities even refuse to reopen the roads until the very last runner has passed, which means that you can be waiting hours for some fat guy who smokes sixty a day or an attention-seeker who insists on running the full 26 miles with 200-pound blocks of concrete strapped to both feet – all in the name of charity of course. If people are so desperate to sponsor someone, can't they just pay you to do your daily commute by car instead?

THIS CARRIAGE SMELLS LIKE A LEBANESE BROTHEL

As you travel to work on a packed commuter train that is standing-room only, you find yourself seduced by that heady aroma of BO and garlic. Searching for words to describe the stench, you soon realize that a wrestler's jockstrap wouldn't do it justice. Nobody around you

seems to have washed under their armpits for at least a
month and the amount of garlic they've all eaten the night
before suggests there must have been reports of vampires
on the loose. The average dog show winner has better
breath. Season tickets are expensive, sure, but do these
people really not have enough money left over for a single
bottle of deodorant or breath freshener?

'But why, oh why, do the wrong
people travel, when the right people stay
back home?'
NOËL COWARD

WHY IS YOUR METER MOVING QUICKER THAN YOUR TAXI?

As soon as you step into a cab, you're in a bad mood. It's
not only because you know that the equivalent journey by
public transport would be about a tenth of the price, but
you look at the meter and find that it's showing £2 before
you've even fastened your seat belt. Of course, it's perfectly
reasonable for cab companies to have a minimum charge
but it's still disconcerting to see that you've paid a tidy

sum of money before you've actually gone anywhere.

So in a bid to keep costs down, you tell the driver the shortest route to your destination because you know full well that, if left to their own devices, most cabbies would take you on the longest route possible.

For the rest of the journey your eyes never stray from the meter, which appears to go round at an alarming pace. Even when the cab is stationary at traffic lights, the meter goes up, which seems grossly unfair. You don't care if the engine's ticking over, you're not moving! Switch the damn thing off if it'll reduce the fare. You're tempted to get out a mile from home and walk the rest of the way just to save money. Yet when you do eventually reach your destination, the driver still expects a tip. Here's one: buy a decent *A to Z*, you miserable sod.

JUST HOW BIG IS YOUR BOTTOM ANYWAY?

Even though they have only bought one ticket, some train passengers seem to believe that permits them to occupy two seats – even if the carriage is crowded. Things like bags of shopping, coats and work files are all piled up on the adjacent seat until some brave soul asks whether the stuff could possibly be moved so that they can sit down. The look of indignation is priceless. After much exaggerated tutting, the pile is slowly moved with a laborious, weary gesture that suggests they had been asked to shift half a dozen bags of wet sand instead of a scarf, a Jackie Collins paperback, and a cheese and pickle sandwich.

What is it about the concept of one ticket equals one seat that these people don't understand? When they buy a house, do they automatically assume it includes the property next door, too?

'You know you're getting old when you start to like your mum and dad again. Yes, Mum, I'd love to come caravanning to Tenby with you. No, I'll bring a packed lunch. I'm not paying café prices.'

JEFF GREEN

MORE ROAD RAGE

Of course, the list is endless. But here are some more things that make you grumpy on the road:

- traffic lights that are on green for five seconds and red for five minutes

- drivers who don't signal before turning but expect you to guess

- tailgaters – the only thing that should ever get that close to your backside is your hand

- Sunday drivers who go really slowly on motorways – they know there's a gas pedal there somewhere but they can't quite remember where

- drivers who take up two parking spaces, because they couldn't quite decide which one to choose

- people who cause chaos by going the wrong way in a parking lot

- drivers who pull out sharply in front of you and then turn off again a hundred yards further down the road

- cyclists – particularly ones who ride two or three abreast because they think they're in the Tour de France

- people who park in disabled bays when they're not disabled . . . yet.

HOW DARE YOU OFFER ME YOUR SEAT?

When you're seventy-five you become grumpy if someone doesn't get up on the bus to offer you their seat. But when you're sixty you become grumpy if someone does get up to offer you their seat. What are they trying to tell you? Damn cheek!

HEY! THAT'S MY PARKING SPOT!

You wait patiently for the lady driver to vacate her parking space. She finds reverse, checks in her mirror for stray eyelashes, wipes a dab of mascara from her cheek, takes a mint from the glove compartment, switches on her iPod, looks in her mirror again to add a touch more lipstick, fast forwards the iPod to her favourite track, edges the car out backwards a foot or so, rummages in her handbag for a tissue, decides she doesn't like that track after all and selects a new one, reverses out a little more, remembers to text her husband to say that she is on her way home, phones her friend to check that dinner's still on for tonight, reverses out completely, decides to switch off the iPod and put the radio on instead, and then drives off. But before you can drive into the space that is rightfully yours, another motorist, newly arrived on the scene, cheekily nips in ahead of you. When you complain that you have been waiting fifteen minutes for that parking spot, he just says, 'Sorry, mate, didn't see you,' and strolls away. Bastard!

Chapter 13

FOOD AND DRINK

HOW ARE YOU SUPPOSED TO OPEN THESE THINGS?

The government are forever warning us about potential hazards to our health and wellbeing – winter flu, bad dietary habits, country and western music – but for some reason this advice has yet to extend to ring pulls on cans. These things are lethal. If you try to open a tin of salmon or a tin of cat food, the ring pull usually either breaks off completely or clamps itself irremovably around your finger. Even in the unlikely event that you do manage to wrench the lid off with the ring pull, you will be left with a deep red wheal in your digit that looks like a failed attempt at amputation. No wonder brown bears prefer to take their chances by attempting to catch the slippery salmon as they leap out of rivers – it's a damn sight easier than mastering ring pulls. And if you think this is an exaggeration, the next time you go to the hospital casualty department just look for the line of middle-aged people waiting with tins of fish stuck to their fingers.

WATCH OUT – THAT LETTUCE COULD BE LETHAL

Now it has officially been recognized that the average American male is approximately the size of Ohio, men all over the world are constantly bombarded with advice about healthy eating. Newspapers love to target us with dietary scare stories, but the findings of these nutritionists are often wildly contradictory. One week, the occasional glass of wine is considered beneficial, the next it can give you everything from diabetes to hard pad. It's the same with chocolate. One week, eating a square of dark chocolate is good for warding off heart attacks, the next it is like signing your own death warrant. How are we supposed to know what to eat when even the so-called experts can't agree? Pass the deep-fried Mars bars.

'Britain is the only country in the world where the food is more dangerous than the sex.'
JACKIE MASON

'Cucumber should be well sliced,
dressed with pepper and vinegar, and
then thrown out, as good for nothing.'
SAMUEL JOHNSON

WAITER! CAN YOU HELP ME FIND MY STEAK?

As you get older, you're forever being told to watch your weight and not eat so much. Certain restaurants play their part in your health kick by giving you smaller portions, although sadly this is never matched by a commensurate reduction in their prices. If you order a steak, it is not unreasonable to expect to spot some part of the cow on your plate. At £15.95 you do not expect to find it hiding coyly beneath a button mushroom or a cherry tomato, afraid to come out in case it's bullied by the onion rings. Where's the rest of it? Is the chef a militant vegetarian?

EVERYTHING WOULD BE FINE IF YOU'D JUST STOP FAWNING OVER ME

Restaurant waiters can take customer service too far. You don't mind being asked once if everything is all right with your meal, but by the time you've been asked the same question by three different members of staff, it becomes rather tiresome. Why do they keep asking whether it's okay? Do they know something that you don't? Are they waiting to see whether you'll discover the dog meat in your lasagne? Their attentiveness has become intrusive. The next thing you know they'll be pulling up a chair and pouring themselves a glass of your wine.

THIS IS A RESTAURANT, NOT A PLAYGROUND FOR DELINQUENT RUGRATS

You go out for a quiet – maybe even romantic – meal, only to find that booked in to the restaurant at the same time as you is a party of ten people, including three noisy toddlers. And because the adults want to drink and chat among themselves, they allow the kids to run about all over the place, squealing with delight and generally spoiling your evening. The waiter may shoot the odd disapproving glare as he trips over a child, nearly giving her a top coat of cream of asparagus soup, but he is too busy to take action.

Inevitably it is only when one of the men in the party has his beer spilled by his wayward infant that the rowdiness suddenly becomes a matter for concern. He immediately instructs his wife to sort it out.

'What am I supposed to do with the kids?' she wails.

At this point you might care to lean over and suggest: 'Have you tried parboiling them?'

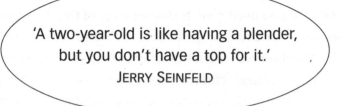

'A two-year-old is like having a blender, but you don't have a top for it.'
JERRY SEINFELD

I'LL CHOOSE MY OWN WORDS, THANKS

A man of mature years should not be expected to have to use terms like Chicken McFlurry – or McSlurry or whatever it is – when ordering in a restaurant. Fast food companies don't realize how demeaning it is for someone who has run his own business, is fluent in four languages and does *The Times* crossword every day to be forced to ask for Tommy Tomato's Super Douper Double Whammy Burger with Extra Scrummy Yummy Cheese. All you really want is a plain burger with cheese, but you're not allowed to ask for that; you have to follow the company terminology.

There was a story recently about a professor who was thrown out of a Manhattan Starbucks because she refused to say that she didn't want butter or cheese on her bagel. She wanted a plain bagel but the waiter wouldn't serve her unless she said 'a bagel with no butter and no cheese'. When she stood firm, tempers became heated and the police were called. She rightly pointed out that when you go into a restaurant you don't give the waiter a list of things you don't want on your bagel or you could be there forever, but in order to get served at that branch it appears that you have to say: 'I'd like a bagel with no butter, no cheese, no onion and while we're at it no soap powder, no iron filings, no gloss paint, no liquid fertilizer, no toothpaste, no haemorrhoid cream and no mouse droppings. You got that?'

I DON'T WANT TO KNOW ITS NAME; I JUST WANT TO EAT IT

Restaurants love to promote organic food, not least because it means they can add 50 per cent to their prices. Playing on your conscience, they give you the entire life history of the lamb as if it were a family pet rather than something you are about to eat. The menu lists its date of birth, family tree, star sign and favourite colour and tells you how it grazed happily in the fields of New Zealand (with a particularly nice view of the snow-capped mountains on a clear day) and spent the evenings sitting around sipping brandy and swapping anecdotes with the rest of the flock. But all this didn't stop it being slaughtered at twelve weeks, did it? Hardly an idyllic life. So spare us the guilt trip, just bring us the mint sauce.

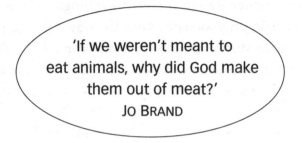

'If we weren't meant to eat animals, why did God make them out of meat?'
JO BRAND

OH NO, WE'VE BEEN INVITED TO A DINNER PARTY

Treated separately, the words 'dinner' and 'party' are fine, but combine them and, rather like 'head butt' or 'American beer', they paint a less attractive picture.

Firstly a dinner party isn't really a party at all. There is rarely any dancing or singing and couples tend not to disappear to the bedroom halfway through the dessert. There is drinking, but it's done at the table while you are seated next to some crashing bore whose talk is so small it is almost microscopic. When you go out for the evening, you want to enjoy yourself – not listen to somebody going on about his office job, his company car and his pension scheme. You get the distinct impression that his idea of a night on the tiles actually involves grouting.

After an evening that seems more like a month, you finally think up an excuse for leaving early, such as 'We're not sure whether we left the bath running,' or 'I need to get home to cut my toenails.' On your way out, you thank the host with stunning insincerity when really you want to quote Groucho Marx by saying: 'I've had a perfectly wonderful evening, but this wasn't it.'

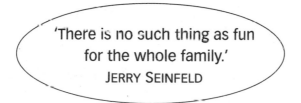

'There is no such thing as fun for the whole family.'
JERRY SEINFELD

DO I LOOK LIKE I NEED A 50-LITRE BUCKET OF POPCORN?

Most cinemas don't allow you to bring in your own food and drink – instead they insist that you buy it on the premises. Fair enough, except all they ever sell are giant versions of everything so that you are forced to part with more money. The bags of sweets are large enough to sustain a family of twelve through the entire *Star Wars* series, the popcorn buckets could feed an army, and the soft drinks come in containers the size of which could flood the Serengeti. By the time you've taken one or more of these into the theatre, there's hardly any room for you to sit, so you end up watching the movie for two and a half hours with your knees squashed up under your chin just to accommodate the Godzilla-sized bag of M&Ms beneath your seat.

I'LL DIE OF STARVATION AT THIS RATE

Opening a packet of biscuits or a bag of sweets should be the easiest thing in the world, because – see! – the manufacturer has added a dotted line on the packaging with the words 'Tear Here'. Except that if you tear exactly where the dotted line is, all you end up with is an unopened packet and sore fingers. What the manufacturer hasn't told you is that to break into the packet you actually need to tear approximately 1 cm to one side or the other of the aforementioned dotted line.

Inevitably the search for the packet's G-Spot leaves you intensely frustrated, with the result that you resort to brute force and no small measure of ignorance and succeed merely in scattering broken biscuits all over the kitchen floor. Then your wife gets so angry with the mess you've made that she puts her back out and ends up in traction, you lose your job because you have to take weeks off work to look after her, the bailiffs repossess your house because without a job you can't keep up with the mortgage payments – and all because manufacturers don't put the dotted line in the right place on the packet.

'Americans can eat garbage, provided you sprinkle it liberally with ketchup, mustard, chilli sauce, Tabasco sauce, cayenne pepper, or any other condiment which destroys the original flavour of the dish.'
HENRY MILLER

Chapter 14

MODERN TRENDS

THE HOLES COST EXTRA

In the old days, if you wore ripped jeans it meant you were either a punk, a hobo or had recently been mauled by a tiger, but now kids pay top prices for a brand-new pair of designer jeans with a huge hole in the knee. Why? These are damaged goods. Would you buy a new coat with a tear in it? Or a pair of shoes with a hole in the toe? Or a new car with the off-side front wing missing? Ripped jeans? Rip-off, more like.

A BUNCH OF TWITS

Twitter seems to have been designed for people with too much time on their hands and an inflated opinion of how interesting their lives are. How else can you explain the need to communicate trivial everyday incidents to the world at large?

Perhaps we should just be grateful that Twitter is a recent invention, otherwise history could have been recorded much differently:

The Battle of Hastings: 'OMG! That SOB Harold has taken 1 in da eye. LOL. NFW back 4 da English now. Will x'

The Monica Lewinsky Affair: 'Soz 4 letting da ppl down. IMO da fing was just inappropriate. Shd no better. H will kill me. Plz 4give. Pres. :('

The Assassination of Julius Caesar: 'TBH will b glad when 2day is over. But it will b gr8 2 c Brutus again – my fav senator. J'

The saddest thing is, soon this may be all that history students will need to know about such events to graduate with honours.

'What the hell is this thing?
I'm supposed to tell you what I'm doing?
Why would I tell you what I'm doing?
What are YOU doing?'
LARRY DAVID ON TWITTER

'The older I get the more I admire and crave competence, just simple competence, in any field from adultery to zoology.'

H. L. MENCKEN

WHY DON'T YOU CHOKE ON YOUR CHILL PILL?

Don't you hate it when someone says patronizingly, 'Chill out, man,' or 'Take a chill pill,' particularly as he or she is invariably the cause of your angst? You think it's a pity their mother didn't take a contraceptive pill, but it's probably best to keep such thoughts to yourself, especially if you want to hold on to your job at the Vatican.

NO-BRAINER? NO BRAIN, MORE LIKE

Of all the daft terms that bounce around business meetings today, a 'no-brainer' is one of the most confusing. If you didn't have a brain, surely your idea would be stupid, whereas a 'no-brainer' actually refers to an idea that is obviously good, i.e. just the opposite. Since most people in business meetings barely have a brain cell between them, they probably haven't noticed the discrepancy.

ARE YOU JUST MAKING UP WORDS NOW?

In modern usage it's not enough to be enthusiastic or overjoyed about something – apparently you have to be 'stoked'. Has nobody explained to people who use this vocabulary that they can only be stoked if they are either a furnace or a total prat? It's not difficult to see which category they fall into. Sadly it's not the furnace.

WHY MUST EVERYBODY HAVE 'ISSUES'?

Once upon a time, only magazines had issues. Now everyone's got them. What used to be simple problems now have to be referred to as 'issues', which makes them sound a hundred times worse. If Little Johnny misbehaves at school, he suddenly has issues with authority. If he struggles to do his sums, he has issues with maths. If he says he doesn't like sausages, he has issues with pork. Of course, if you disagree with any of this idiotic claptrap, you have issues with people who say that others have issues. But that's another issue altogether.

WHO'S THE BUFFOON IN THE BASEBALL CAP?

Baseball caps on young people are absolutely fine. Baseball caps on older people are generally ill-advised, even if they do hide that unsightly bald patch. But a politician wearing a baseball cap is, like passing gas in an elevator, wrong on so many levels. It smacks of a desperate attempt to engage with young voters, particularly, as in the case of forty-nine-year-old Foreign Secretary William Hague in 2010, when accompanied by wraparound sunglasses. He couldn't have looked less dignified had he been wearing Mickey Mouse ears. The result was a total loss of credibility, and with politicians that commodity is in short supply anyway. Would anyone have taken Lincoln seriously if he had given the Gettysburg Address speech wearing a baseball cap? Would Gandhi have been treated with the same reverence had he taken to sporting a hoodie and a phat gold chain? Like breakdancing, skateboarding and membership of the Hannah Montana fan club, some things are simply best left to the young.

'I don't care for modern films.
Cars crashing over cliffs and close-ups
of people's feet.'
LILLIAN GISH

SENDING A MAN INTO SPACE? IT'S NOT ROCKET SCIENCE.

Well, yes it is actually. So you'll have to find some other way of being unimaginatively condescending.

A DEGREE IN IDLING FROM THE UNIVERSITY OF S.O.F.A. IS NOT A REAL QUALIFICATION, YOU KNOW

In our day we studied proper subjects at college and university, but now kids can get diplomas or degrees in things like hairdressing, tourism and nail technology. The University of South Carolina is even offering a course in Lady Gaga, which begs the question: who's gaga – her or the university?

The media call them Mickey Mouse degrees, which would be laughable except for the fact that there is probably a university somewhere offering a course in Disney studies. These soft options may be relatively easy to pass but they don't necessarily help kids get a job. That's why they are then forced to deal with crushing disappointment when, armed with their degree in media studies, they find they're not editing *The Times* or presenting on primetime television six months later.

Soon these subjects will probably be offered for degree courses at a university near you:

- paintballing

- flower arranging

- Nintendo Wii

- rock-paper-scissors

- advanced tree climbing

- the shipping forecast

- Ker-plunk

- setting the DVD recorder (actually, this last one might be useful).

'The telephone is a good way to talk to people without having to offer them a drink.'
FRAN LEBOWITZ

HELP, MY DAUGHTER HAS TURNED INTO BRIDEZILLA

The greatest financial concern among middle-aged men is not whether they have put aside sufficient money in case of unexpected redundancy or ill health, it's whether they have saved up enough to pay for their daughter's wedding. The average American wedding costs $20,000 – and that's before the honeymoon – and includes such essentials as teeth whitening for the bride, gym sessions so that she can fit into her dress, a massage to keep her calm and focused, and dance lessons for both bride and groom so that they don't fall flat on their faces at the reception. Why not add cake-cutting lessons to ensure that they don't accidentally stab the best man while slicing through the wedding cake or juggling lessons so that they can find a use for the three electric toasters which they will inevitably receive?

The groom's interest in the wedding arrangements rarely extends beyond the stag night and making sure there's plenty of beer at the reception. Should a TV set be visible so that he can watch the football results during the father-of-the-bride's speech, then the day would be just about perfect. The bride, however, couldn't possibly be happy unless she has emptied her father's bank account on everything from hiring David Bailey as the wedding photographer to having initialized gold-embossed napkins. If her father plucks up the courage to ask her why she needs such an expensive wedding, she says: 'Because it's the biggest, most important day in my life.' Sure, until constant rows about her spending mean she's planning her divorce eighteen months later.

HAVEN'T THESE PEOPLE GOT ANYTHING BETTER TO DO?

In order to maintain their government funding, universities are obliged to produce various theses on topics of national and international importance. At the leading universities these works often have genuine worth, making discoveries that can shape the future, but at some of the lesser institutions the emphasis seems to be on stating the bleeding obvious. For example, Japanese scientists spent seven years on a study before concluding that earthquakes are not caused by catfish wiggling their tails. You don't say! Meanwhile academics across the globe can spend months of dedicated research before concluding that:

- yes, it hurts if you whack your knee with a hammer

- it is the physiology of a giant tortoise that prevents it from running at 70 mph

- fire is dangerous.

When they're not reaching such earth-shattering conclusions, the finest brains in the land are producing lengthy theses on subjects that nobody gives a damn about anyway, such as:

- developing a magnet strong enough to levitate a frog

- discovering that fleas that live on a dog can jump higher than fleas that live on a cat

- calculating how long it would take a centipede to walk around the world if he started and finished in New York and called in at every capital city on the way.

Give these people something useful to do instead – something that is more suited to their talents, like sweeping the corridors.

'Nothing matters very much, and few things matter at all.'
THE EARL OF BALFOUR

'All marriages are happy.
It's the living together afterward
that causes all the trouble.'
RAYMOND HULL

REPETITION, REPETITION, REPETITION

Repeats have always been part of the TV schedules but at least channels used to have the decency to wait a few months before showing reruns. Now you can often watch the same programme three times in the space of three days – first the original show, then an extended version of that show (with 'hilarious' out-takes), and finally a repeat of the original. And all this at a time when virtually every home in the land has either a DVD recorder or a video recorder. Basically the schedulers are just offering you another chance to miss a programme you didn't want to watch in the first place.

MODERN ART IS RUBBISH

As yet nobody has explained satisfactorily how an unmade bed, a light switching on and off and a heap of dust can be regarded as works of art. At school if you'd piled a load of old cartons, wrappers, empty bottles and scraps of newspaper in a corner and told the teacher it was art, you'd have been put in detention for a week and told to clean up the mess.

But all over the world, city councils, even in times of severe economic cutbacks, are spending thousands of pounds on sculptures that appear to have been created by a gorilla with learning difficulties. When asked whether the money could not have been better spent elsewhere, they counter that the sculpture will bring pleasure to many, many people. In fact, the only people to whom it does bring pleasure are the kids who spray graffiti on it within a week.

Every year there are stories about gallery cleaners accidentally throwing out a supposedly valuable piece of modern art because they thought it was just trash. There's a reason for that: it's because it is just trash.

NO, YOU GET IN THE HOLE

If playing golf is too energetic at your age, you can always watch it on TV, where the gentle pace of play, the lush greens, the lapping of waves on the seashore and the sound of birdsong make it a thoroughly relaxing experience. You may even stay awake for some of it. Alas, in recent years TV coverage has been spoiled by those mindless morons who follow the players around the course and yell 'Get in the hole!' after each shot.

Almost inevitably it was a trend that originated in the United States but it was quickly adopted by British spectators eager not to be outdone in the 'complete numbskull' stakes. One can almost accept the cry as little more than over-enthusiasm when it follows the striking of a putt, but when it accompanies a tee shot on a 525-yard par-5, it is ridiculous beyond parody. You almost feel sorry for the golfers themselves, having to listen to such drivel throughout their round. Tiger Woods must wake up in the night yelling 'Get in the hole', but then again it probably wasn't golf he was dreaming about.

IF YOU'RE A CELEBRITY, PLEASE GET OUT OF HERE

Whenever you go on the computer to check whether you've got another email from that nice man in Nigeria promising you $250,000 if you just give him your credit card number and bank details, you are immediately greeted with the latest non-story about some young Z-list celebrity whose number of marriages is outstripped only by the number of volumes of her autobiography. There will be an accompanying picture of her climbing out of a taxi or falling out of a nightclub, for that is her sole talent: an ability to be photographed. She can't sing, she can't act – hell, she can't even tap dance or play a decent tune on the accordion! So what has she done to make the headlines this time? Her friends fear for her health because she's broken a toenail.

SCHOOL REPORTS: COULD DO BETTER

When we were kids, a bit of discipline at school never hurt us. Well, apart from the cane – that hurt quite a bit, as did a blackboard rubber when it was hurled at you by a homicidal geography teacher. But now teachers aren't allowed to discipline kids at all. They can't string them up from the beams of the school gym, they can't tell them off, and they can't even say anything negative about them.

Consequently the kids' school reports say things like:

- Darren continues to make excellent progress. Even the petrol bomb he made for his arson attack on the school chemistry laboratory was well planned, using all the right substances. Well done!

- Jamie's eye for a business opportunity has again impressed us all – his protection racket goes from strength to strength.

- Jade's ingenuity at taking Mr Simpson's briefcase and photocopying the exam questions beforehand ensured that she got top marks. Keep up the good work!

- Glossing over the unfortunate incident with Mr Kelly – and he does still have one good eye – Sharlene remains a lively member of class with a challenging, enquiring mind. She has shown great initiative this term by forming her own gang.

Apparently it's all about boosting their confidence so that when they leave school they'll be able to climb to the very top of their chosen career, which in many cases will mean armed robbery.

EVEN MAN-EATING SHARKS HAVE STANDARDS, YOU KNOW

We've had TV shows featuring minor celebrities in a house, in the jungle, in the Arctic, on an island, cooking, dancing, singing, ice skating, riding horses, boxing, losing weight, and training dogs – but sadly none where a celebrity has faced an agonizing death. So the only new celebrity TV series that should be commissioned is one where a dozen of them are coated in eau de mackerel and thrown to great white sharks. The winner would be the one who is regurgitated the fastest, because feared predators though they may be, not even sharks can stomach former *Big Brother* contestants.

SINCE WHEN HAVE WOMEN BECOME 'GUYS'?

Another irritating phrase is the apparent need to address everyone – male and female – as 'you guys'. This greeting is particularly prevalent among waiters at those modern bar-diners. They see you sitting at a table with five female colleagues and ask: 'What would you guys like to order?'

You look around at the others and think: 'Well, I know Jane from Human Resources has a little dark facial hair, which, with careful grooming, might one day make an excellent Zapata moustache, but at the moment there is no way that she could be mistaken for a man. Equally Monica from Marketing should not be considered a man simply because she has short hair, drinks pints and has implausibly small breasts.'

So why call them 'guys'? Middle-aged men are perfectly happy to be referred to as 'guys' because it makes them sound young, cool and hip, although their wives will tell them that the real reason they look like a guy is that they're wearing scruffy old clothes, are worth no more than a penny and only go out once a year – and even then they have to be carried back home.

The fact is, only men should be called 'guys'. Even a San Francisco waiter would hesitate at calling two burly male builders 'you chicks', so let's put a stop to this crazy gender confusion before the remake of *Guys and Dolls* becomes a lesbian extravaganza.

BUT YOU'RE STOPPING ME FROM HAVING A NICE DAY

For centuries, people have been perfectly happy bidding each other a polite 'good morning'. But now the language is assailed with people exhorting us to 'have a nice day', which is not so much an expression of hope as a command. 'You will have a nice day, and if you don't you'll be hearing from our lawyers.'

This tedious greeting is trotted out relentlessly by store staff and customer services workers, seemingly oblivious to the fact that they are often the very ones who prevent us from having a nice day. 'Sorry I can't refund you the cost of the train ticket that you were unable to use through no fault of your own. Never mind, eh? Have a nice day.'

AT LAST! A SOCIAL GROUP I CAN JOIN!

For those of us who are fed up with all these social networking sites and don't want to acquire dozens of new 'friends', maybe it's time to start up an antisocial networking site. It could be called Shutyerfacebook.

I'D RATHER NOT SPEND A PENNY, THANKS

There are a number of advantages to being a man. For example, we can eat a banana in public, we can complete a phone call in thirty seconds, the same hairstyle lasts us for years, and if another guy shows up at a party wearing the same outfit, we might even become lifelong friends. Another plus is that we don't have to queue for public toilets.

Nor until recent years did we have to pay to use them. Women did, but also they had to queue for ages. For them, using a public toilet was – and still is – only marginally less traumatic than giving birth, but for us men it was a stroll in the park, which, coincidentally, was where we'd often go if the toilets were closed. For men, the world is our urinal. So the thought of suddenly having to pay to use the toilet came as a body blow.

It's not so bad if you need to do number twos because a nice clean seat and plenty of smooth paper – coupled with the relief – make it money well spent. But to pay in order to pee on a pile of cigarette butts and a stale toilet freshener represents worse value than offering Sarah Palin a penny for her thoughts.

HEY FATSO, WHAT DO YOU MEAN I'M NOT POLITICALLY CORRECT?

Aren't you sick of all the politically correct terminology whereby someone who is ignorant has to be called 'factually unencumbered', a pig-ugly person is described as 'cosmetically different' and someone who is dishonest is instead called 'ethically disoriented'? A gravitationally challenged (fat) lot of good it does!

The idea is to spare the feelings of sensitive souls, but do the politically correct brigade really think a lazy person is bothered whether or not he is called 'motivationally deficient' and that a cannibal is going to spare you from the cooking pot just because you call him an 'intra-species diner'?

It's enough to make you 'experience an unplanned re-examination of recent food choices' (sick).

SILENCE ON COURT!

There is a place for women to grunt and groan, but it's on an adult movie channel – not on a tennis court. Yet so many leading female players seem incapable of hitting a shot without making a noise like a rutting stag. The number of decibels produced by Serena Williams has been compared to that of a jumbo jet, although that's not necessarily where the similarity between the two ends.

Is it just an affectation or is it gamesmanship designed to put off their opponent? One or two are scary enough anyway without needing sound effects. Does it carry over into everyday life? Does Monica Seles moan while doing the washing up? Plenty of men do.

'Abstract art? A product of the untalented sold by the unprincipled to the utterly bewildered.'
AL CAPP

CALL THE POLICE – I'VE BEEN TAGGED AND POKED

Social networking sites are all the rage – Facebook alone has more than 500 million users – but does sitting in front of a computer all evening really constitute a friendship? Wouldn't it be better to talk to your friends in person, or has the art of conversation been replaced by a keyboard?

According to your personal web page, your popularity is such that you make Justin Timberlake look like Billy No-mates. Apparently you have dozens of 'friends', but who are these people? You wouldn't recognize them from Adam. Do they all expect to be invited round for drinks and canapés? Where were they when your wife left you and your house was repossessed? What would they say if you asked them to lend you £20?

The fact is they've only become your 'friend' because in your list of personal interests you mentioned that you like tennis and so do they. Does this mean that Roger Federer is your friend, too? Will you get a birthday card this year from Andy Roddick? Thought not. Well, you're not my friend any more, Andy.

Chapter 15

THE INSOLENCE OF YOUTH

The youth of today seem to think that just because you're not dropping litter and spitting in the street you're over the hill. And, while their own vocabulary rarely extends beyond a grunt, they've devised an entire dictionary of derogatory terms for anyone old enough to drive. These may be upsetting but, in the belief that forewarned is forearmed, it is important for you to know exactly what insults are out there. Helpfully, each insult has been given an 'old git' rating of between 1 and 5, ranging from mildly offensive to worth launching a retaliatory attack with a sharpened umbrella.

OLD FART

Immortalized by former England rugby captain Will Carling, who denounced the executive of the Rugby

Football Union as 'fifty-seven old farts', the term is generally linked to upper-class senior men who belong to private clubs, smoke fat cigars and are completely clueless. The association is appropriate because old farts are all hot air, they make a lot of noise, lack any sense of direction, and create a stink.

Old Git Rating: 4

OLD GIT

Not technically an insult, though used as one, an old git is traditionally a grumpy senior who hates everything and everyone, from Christmas to Bambi. Statler and Waldorf from *The Muppet Show* were old gits.

Old Git Rating: 3

CRUSTY

A crusty has hygiene as well as age issues. To call someone a crusty is to question his personal cleanliness, the word itself referring to the likely state of his underwear. A crusty will invariably have food on his tie, soup down his trousers and a three-course meal in his beard. A crusty treats a bar of soap like an arachnophobic treats a tarantula. Note that the world's most famous crusty – the clown from *The Simpsons* – deliberately spells his name with a K, although this could have something to do with the fact that his real name is Herschel Krustofski.

Old Git Rating: 5

WRINKLY

Sometimes given the prefix 'old' just to emphasize the point, this is probably the most common term of abuse you are likely to have hurled at you, although the development of Botox has seen a decline in the number of genuine wrinklies, at least among the celebrity set. The ultimate wrinkly is the Galapagos Giant Tortoise and it can live for over 200 years, which is ample compensation for having skin like Michael Parkinson.

Old Git Rating: 5

'People who hate children
and small dogs can't be all bad.'
W.C. FIELDS

CODGER

A contraction of 'coffin dodger', this term usually implies a form of elderly cunning and is therefore less objectionable than many others. Someone who jumps the queue at the Post Office on the pretence that their old war wound is playing up or who erects tripwires at skateboard parks might be described as a codger. Extreme codgers end up being sought on Most Wanted.

Old Git Rating: 2

GERIATRIC

Once purely a medical term (from the Greek word *geras* meaning 'old age'), geriatric is often used to deride the oldest and most infirm. If you are in your thirties or forties and someone calls you geriatric, you should consult either a doctor or a lawyer. Teenagers often condense this to 'gerro' since they can't be expected to master any word that has four syllables.

Old Git Rating: 4

DINOSAUR

The term 'dinosaur' is used to mock a mindset rather than physical appearance – unless you happen to be 8 feet tall with a small head, long tail and scaly skin. Typically a dinosaur is someone that lives in the past, who yearns for the days of powdered egg and Prohibition, reckons that television programmes were better in black and white, and believes that the crime rate would be drastically reduced by the reintroduction of the rack. 'Fossil' or 'old fogey' – or even 'old git' – can be used to similar effect.

Old Git Rating: 3

'Two things should be cut:
the second act and the child's throat.'
NOËL COWARD,
REFERRING TO A CHILD ACTOR

MOULDY

If teenagers can merge two words into one, they will because it requires less effort. So rather than refer to their parents as 'mouldy oldies', they contract it to 'mouldies'. The term is not hugely derogatory, merely indicative of the way teens see their parents – i.e. outdated and pointless, until it comes to paying for their dream wedding.

Old Git Rating: 2

DUFFER

Similar to a dodderer, a duffer is an old fool who really shouldn't be allowed out without supervision. Duffers take five minutes to step off a kerb and rarely exceed 15 mph at the wheel of a car. Fortunately they avoid motorways, considering them to be the tool of the devil. Duffers are easily recognized in supermarkets by the trail of smashed eggs, broken jars and squashed tomatoes they leave in their wake.

Old Git Rating: 2

CROC FACE

Crocodiles are known neither for their youthful-looking skin nor their sensitivity, so to be called 'croc face' is less than flattering. Just as an old crocks' race features vintage cars, so an old croc face refers to someone possessing a vintage countenance. You could be upset by the insult or, like a true crocodile, you could just snap out of it.

Old Git Rating: 5

GRANDAD

'Grandad' can be a wounding insult if you're thirty-seven and going prematurely grey, bald or both. Otherwise it is relatively mild, although grandads can also be a bit clumsy, displaying the handling dexterity of a twice-convicted Arabian shoplifter.

Old Git Rating: 2

'The nice thing about having relatives' kids around is that they go home.'
CLIFF RICHARD

BEDBLOCKER

A bedblocker is a person who occupies a hospital bed for an inordinately long time, thereby preventing younger, supposedly worthier cases from receiving treatment. If a nurse accuses you of being a malingering bedblocker, prove that you really are ill by vomiting your dinner over her. Given all the superbugs circulating on the wards, that shouldn't be difficult.

Old Git Rating: 4

Should you be subjected to any of the above taunts, you could point out to your tormentors that despite your 'seniority' you have acquired a depth of social understanding and academic qualifications far beyond their comprehension. Alternatively you could just yell 'knobhead' and move on.

Chapter 16

LINE THEM UP AGAINST A WALL ...

Some groups of people are so annoying that you're tempted to think the only way to deal with them satisfactorily is by firing squad. That may be a little extreme, but only just.

IF ONLY WE STILL HAD SILENT MOVIES

Why do people pay good money to see a movie and then talk the whole way through it? It is so distracting. You find that one ear is listening to the on-screen action and the other to the conversation behind you. The two can become muddled so that while watching an espionage thriller you end up convinced that the CIA assassin was 'cousin Margery who breeds rabbits – you know, Paul's daughter'.

If a stage play is interrupted by constant chatter among the audience, the cast are likely to admonish them, but – alas – in a cinema there is little chance of Bruce Willis bursting through the screen and throttling the guy in the third row of the stalls for talking throughout his big scene.

Which is a shame.

YES, I DO MIND IF YOU PUSH IN AHEAD OF ME

When a little old lady sidles up to you in the queue at the supermarket or the bank with a pleading look in her eyes, you know instinctively what's coming. 'Do you mind if I go first?' she asks innocently. 'I'll only be a moment and I've got a bus to catch/a doctor's appointment/severe flatulence.'

Not wishing to appear the grumpy old git that you really are, you grudgingly let her go in front of you, only to discover that while she does indeed only have one item or a simple request, she knows the cashier personally. Consequently they spend the next thirty minutes chatting away merrily about mutual friends, how the garden is looking and the price of cheese until it's time for the cashier to go on her break and put up the 'Till Closed' sign.

'I sometimes think that God,
in creating man, somewhat
overestimated His ability.'
OSCAR WILDE

WHAT DO YOU MEAN, I'M NOT GOING TO SCORE THE WINNING GOAL IN THE CUP FINAL?

Self-empowerment books: the shelves are full of them, each promising the answer to achieving wealth, health and general fulfilment in life. Cutting through the scientific mumbo-jumbo that these authors roll out to disguise the fact that you are paying £12 for a very thin idea, the basic premise is: if you wish for something hard enough you will get it. This, they tell you, is how Edison invented the light bulb, how Wellington defeated Napoleon at Waterloo and how Kerry Katona continues to be famous despite no discernable talent.

Positive thinking is one thing, but to say all your dreams will come true if you just want something badly enough is stretching credibility to breaking point. In your younger days, you may desperately have wanted to go on a date with Brigitte Bardot, but what did you get? Nothing. Not a phone call, not a letter, not even a knowing wink on screen in *Viva Maria!* It's the same nowadays with the lottery. Every week, millions of people across the world really, really want to win their national lottery, but only a handful ever do. For the remainder, self-empowerment, like the lottery itself, is just a load of balls.

In fact the only people for whom self-empowerment seems to work are the authors of books on the subject who make enough money from gullible readers to keep themselves in energy beads for life.

'Life is divided into the horrible and the miserable.'
WOODY ALLEN, IN *ANNIE HALL*

YOU MIGHT BE ENJOYING YOUR MEAL, BUT WE'RE NOT

Watching someone eat with their mouth open is like seeing a washing machine on spin cycle – but with pieces of masticated pork in place of clothes and saliva instead of soapsuds. Camels manage to eat with their mouth closed

– although they do tend to foam a bit around the lips, which it has to be said is not an overly attractive habit – so why can't humans? Let's face it, you don't want to see the contents of someone's mouth any more than you want to see what's in their small intestine.

IT'S NOT THAT HARD TO SWALLOW, YOU KNOW

Isn't it curious how some sportsmen – footballers and baseball players in particular – spend an hour or so warming up for the game but wait until they actually run out on to the pitch in front of thousands of spectators before deciding to spit? But do they make up for lost time! Some spit out so much phlegm that you fear the pitch will become waterlogged.

Is it absolutely necessary? Surely there must be a suitable receptacle in the dressing room for excess mucus. Or do they get some kick out of doing it in public, like couples who have sex in shop windows?

Thankfully a few, less energetic sports are still free of the spitting curse. We have yet to encounter wholesale gobbing in golf, bowls or indeed chess where it would be bordering on gamesmanship to cause your opponent's rook to slide off the board on a sea of spit.

SMOKING AND DRINKING BORES CAN CAUSE YOU TO KILL

Possibly the only thing worse than being trapped in the company of someone who smokes like a chimney is being trapped in the company of an ex-smoker. They might not kill you with their fumes but they'll sure as hell bore you to death. For they've seen the light, they've been spared, they're the chosen ones, and now they see it as their duty to preach to anyone and everyone about the perils of smoking. But you don't want – or need – to be preached at because like most people you had the good sense not to smoke forty a day in the first place.

What do they want? A medal? It's like a released axe murderer expecting praise just because he hasn't hacked anyone to death for three months.

Reformed alcoholics are equally as bad with their determination to convert you to their way of life. They warn you that drink is evil, the tool of the devil, and they cannot accept your protestations that half a shandy two nights a week is unlikely to turn you into Charlie Sheen.

'And a woman is only a woman,
but a good cigar is a smoke.'
RUDYARD KIPLING

Edmund Blackadder: 'What on earth was I drinking last night? My head feels like there's a Frenchman living in it.'
RICHARD CURTIS AND BEN ELTON, WRITERS OF *BLACKADDER*

I ONLY EAT THINGS WITH A FACE

As if reformed smokers and alcoholics weren't bad enough, heaven help you if you ever find yourself entertaining some vegetarians – or even worse, vegans, the provisional wing of vegetarians. If you do, try saying one of the following to get rid of them:

- It's against my religion to eat anything that didn't once have parents.

- If God had intended cod or haddock for any purpose other than to be eaten, He would have made them better looking.

- How can you eat potatoes, knowing that they have eyes?

- How can you possibly eat sweetcorn, when you know it has ears?

- How can you bear to eat lettuce? They have hearts, you know.

- How on earth can you eat lentils, when they taste like shite?

A SIMPLE 'THANK YOU' WOULDN'T HURT

When you demonstrate good manners by holding the door open for someone, it should not be too much effort for the other person to reciprocate by saying 'thank you'. It's not the most demanding of responses – you're not expecting a witty Wildean rejoinder. But instead some people swan through without a nod or a word as if they were Hollywood royalty and you were the doorman. These people deserve a sharp kick up the tradesman's entrance.

'I knew I was going bald when it was taking longer and longer to wash my face.'
HARRY HILL

THESE AREN'T WRINKLES: MY SKIN IS JUST TOO BIG FOR MY FACE

As men get older, it is not uncommon for them to develop a deep dislike – sometimes bordering on hatred – of other men who look impossibly young for their age. For when you look in the mirror at a head so bald you could play air hockey on it, a face so wrinkled you could pass for a prune, eyes which have not just got bags under them but suitcases, and so many double chins that it looks as though you're peering over a pile of pancakes, it is hard not to feel jealous of men who look much the same in their sixties as they did in their twenties and thirties.

Since a fresh, youthful face is but a distant memory to most men by the time they've reached thirty, it should be against the law for a chosen few to defy the ravages of time. It's not your fault that your bones are so creaky that when you get up in the morning it sounds as if you're making popcorn. It's just natural ageing, which is more than can be said for a sixty-something who uses so much gel that he can't let his hair down without three days' notice and who has had so many facelifts that every time he smiles his toes wiggle.

At least you can console yourself with the fact that what looks you have are all your own and haven't come out of a catalogue.

The Grumpy Old Git's Guide to Life

YOU'RE NOT THE FIRST WOMAN TO GIVE BIRTH, YOU KNOW!

Men and women don't always see eye to eye but one thing on which there is almost universal agreement is our shared distaste for celebrity first-time mothers. Sure, these people are overjoyed at becoming a mum but by the way they carry on you would think that nobody had ever given birth before. Over 200,000 women give birth every day, but they don't all bring out step-by-step books and DVDs or have lucrative magazine deals promoting the new placenta perfume range they've launched.

And then these celebrity supermums show what an inspiration they are to the ordinary woman in the street by getting their figures back and returning to work within a week. How do they manage that, you ask in wonderment? Because they dump the baby with a twenty-four-hour rota of nannies, pay a small fortune to their personal trainer/ plastic surgeon to sort out their mummy tummies, then take a chauffeur-driven limo to the nearest TV studios to tell the world how motherhood has really, you know, grounded them.

174

HELL IS OTHER PEOPLE

If you're not wound up enough already, consider the following walking nightmares:

- people who use their credit card in busy bars to buy one drink

- people who don't fold road maps properly

- people who refer to themselves in the third person

- people who give their children stupid names like Pilot Inspektor, Princess Tiamii, Moxie CrimeFighter, Heavenly Hiraani Tiger Lily, Audio Science and Apple

- people who tell you: 'I hear what you say'

- people who put apostrophe's in the wrong place

- people who keep pressing elevator buttons in the belief that it will make the doors close quicker

- pedestrians who stop dead in the street right in front of you, without warning

- salespeople who say 'no obligation' but then bombard you with calls for the next three months

- people who have ridiculous novelty ringtones on their mobile phones

- people with overblown job titles

- anyone called Wayne.

HIS NICKNAME IS 'PROCTOLOGIST' BECAUSE HE'S SO FAR UP THE BOSS'S BACKSIDE

There is nothing worse than sharing an office with someone who constantly crawls to the boss – especially if he's better at it than you are. The majority of these creeps are just irritating, although someone who goes around with a pair of scissors cutting the boss's wife out of all photographs of the couple may be seen as perhaps a little too ambitious.

How to spot someone who crawls to the boss:

- He laughs at all the boss's jokes.

- He stays late in the office every night – until the precise moment the boss's limo has left the car park.

- He remembers the boss's birthday.

- He remembers the boss's wife's birthday, and those of their three children.

- He buys the boss a cup of tea – but nobody else.

- He compliments the boss on his new tie – even though it is pink with brown spots and a picture of Dolly Parton.

- He has been caught rubbing himself on the corner of the boss's desk.

- He only ever volunteers to buy a round of drinks at the bar when the boss is there.

- He has a brown mark on the end of his nose.

SCOOP THAT POOP

Of all the idle people in the world, among the laziest are those who can't be bothered to clean up their dog's mess. All it needs is a plastic scooper and a bag to make the pavement fit for others to walk on, instead of having to play hopscotch to avoid strategically placed piles of dog poop. Street corners are the worst. No dog seems able to take a corner without doing a dump. It makes you wonder how greyhounds manage to complete a lap without taking toilet breaks.

If you challenge a dog owner over their lack of clearing-up equipment, they'll say something like: 'Sorry, but I wasn't expecting him to do anything.'

What do they mean they weren't expecting him to do anything? That's the whole purpose of him going for a walk – to do a poop. He doesn't go for a walk to smell the roses or admire the architecture. Next time you catch a dog fouling the footpath, perhaps you should bring your pet to cr*p outside their house. Come here, Jumbo . . .

'I'm free of all prejudices.
I hate everyone equally.'
W.C. FIELDS

HOW DO I GET TO BE AN OVERPAID BUSINESS CONSULTANT?

Apart from hospitals where they perform a valuable function, it is hard to think of any business whose efficiency has been enhanced by the services of consultants. Pinpointing what consultants actually do is like trying to nail blancmange but basically they are paid a great deal of money to give companies advice that their own employees should know anyway. Anyone with the slightest knowledge of a subject can set up as a consultant. So King Herod could have become a paediatric consultant, the Boston Strangler could have become a mortuary consultant, and Desperate Dan could set up as a dietary consultant. And Tony Blair could become a peace consultant/envoy to the Middle East – but no, that would be too far-fetched.

JOG OFF

You're enjoying a leisurely morning stroll when you hear the sound of puffing and panting behind you. You turn around to see some wheezing fellow, his face as red as his vest, bearing down on you. Is he going to run around you like any civilized human being? Of course not, because he's a jogger.

Put a jogger on a footpath or pavement and he immediately assumes the mantle of a truck driver on a highway – he thinks everyone should move out of his way. 'Hey, I'm a serious athlete,' he will say. 'To break stride will ruin my training.'

But joggers are to serious athletics what crazy golf is to the Ryder Cup. Most people can walk faster than joggers jog. Half the time they seem to be going up and down on the spot, on the brink of collapse. So why should you step aside onto muddy grass just to let them through? The Olympics will just have to get by without them.

IF YOU REALLY WANT SOMETHING TO CRY ABOUT, I'M SURE WE CAN HELP . . .

When a celebrity appears on a TV chat show these days, it's a safe bet that he or she will burst into tears at least once in the course of the interview. Particularly if they have a new book/album/fragrance/range of clothes to promote or are desperate for public sympathy following a media mauling, they are prone to sobbing uncontrollably at the first sign of a camera. Some female celebrities publicly shed their body weight in tears every week.

People in the real world have to deal with crises on a daily basis but they usually manage to keep their emotions in check, so why do celebrities feel the need to turn on the waterworks over the most trivial of matters? Do they really think the public can't see through their crocodile tears?

Here are just a few of the many things that make today's celebrities cry:

- not being featured in *OK!* magazine for three whole weeks

- stepping out of the house in the morning to find the only photographer is an estate agent taking a picture of the property next door

- breaking up with someone who could have been beneficial to their career

- a newspaper or magazine printing their real age

- the posting of 'intrusive, embarrassing' photos of them on the Internet before they have had the chance to sell the same pictures to a national newspaper for a six-figure sum

- the remaindering of their autobiography

- learning that another celebrity has adopted more Third World babies than they have.

Celebrities who cry in public: line them up against a wall.

Chapter 17

THINK YOU'VE GOT IT BAD?

Sometimes, when it's grey outside, your boiler's on the blink and some call-centre eejit just rang to sell you something you already own, the only thing worth living for is the news of other people's misfortunes. If you think everything is s**t, take comfort from these edifying tales of idiocy.

- A jogger who took a wrong turn during his regular lunchtime run in Florida ended up stuck in a swamp for four days. Training for the 2006 Baltimore Marathon, Eddie Meadows left his desk at the University of Central Florida's research park every lunchtime to jog around the campus, but on this occasion he became hopelessly lost and fell into a bog.

- Christine Jenkins, a forty-nine-year-old Berkshire woman who enjoyed a night of passion at a wealthy stranger's luxurious home in 2004 after meeting him in a nightclub, woke in the king-size bed the next morning to find her lover gone but three people staring at her. They were the estate agent and two prospective buyers for the show house.

- Wanting a gas stove for her apartment, Loretta Mason of San Francisco, California, stole one from a neighbouring building in 2003 . . . without first turning off the gas. Her oversight caused a $200,000 explosion.

- In 1996, William Alexander, a former traffic policeman, set out to drive the 15 miles from Hereford to Ross-on-Wye. He and his wife were found confused thirty-six hours later, after a 1,000-mile drive, going the wrong way down the M1 near Barnsley.

- Teachers at a Belgian nursery school panicked in 2007 after a man who came to pick up his granddaughter accidentally took home the wrong girl. With a search underway, police received a call from Fernand Etienne, sixty, to say that his wife had told him the little girl he had collected was not their granddaughter Marie.

- A year after crashing into Jim Hughes's yacht near Portsmouth and causing £20,000 damage, Icelandic sailor Eriker Olafsson still felt guilty. So he decided to return to the harbour and apologize, only to hit Mr Hughes's yacht again and postpone his plans for a round-the-world voyage for a second time.

- When Ivo Jerbic from Prikraj, Croatia, couldn't find any clean underpants, he angrily set fire to his clothes in the garden and accidentally burnt his house down.

- Eighty-three-year-old Maurice Vernon from British Columbia, Canada, failed his driving exam in 2001 after confusing the accelerator with the brake and reversing his car through the window of the test centre.

- A newly married Romanian farmer fractured his penis in 2005 after ogling his young wife while carrying a heavy sack of grain. Gheorghe Popa, fifty-two, stopped work to watch his twenty-five-year-old bride Loredana hang up some washing but became over-excited and dropped the sack on his erect organ, snapping vital tendons and ligaments.

- An eighty-four-year-old woman nearly burned down her old folks' home in 2007 after putting her slippers under the grill to warm them up. Joan Hiscock forgot all about the slippers until they caught fire, forcing dozens of residents to be evacuated from the sheltered accommodation in Stockbridge, Hampshire. When nine firefighters raced to the scene to put out the blaze, they found the smouldering slippers on the grill pan.

- Ken Barger of Newton, North Carolina, accidentally shot himself dead in 1992 while answering the phone in the middle of the night. Barger went to pick up the phone beside his bed but, half asleep, grabbed his .38 Smith and Wesson special instead. The gun went off when he pulled it to his ear.

- Mr Cui, a businessman from Qingdao, China, was so concerned about the possibility of burglars while he and his wife were away on a business trip that he took the precaution of hiding their $6,400 savings in the garbage bin. But on his return from the trip he forgot all about the money and put it out for collection with the rest of the garbage. By the time he realized his oversight, his hard-earned cash had been irretrievably buried in a landfill site.

- Barry and Carol Watson of Cliftonville, Kent, booked a round-the-world trip to celebrate their silver wedding anniversary, only to discover that they were a year too early. Having spent two years planning the trip, they went ahead with it anyway and were showered with gifts wherever they travelled but were too embarrassed to admit they had really only been married for twenty-four years.

- Two old-timers from Cleveland, Ohio, who decided to settle a long-standing feud with a gun duel in their apartment block, survived the experience without so much as a graze. Armed with antique pistols, the pair stood 5 feet apart in the hallway separating their apartments and each fired twelve bullets. Every shot hopelessly missed its target but left the walls peppered with bullet holes. Police officers speculated that the lack of accuracy may have been due to the fact that one antagonist needed a stick to prop himself up while firing and the other had difficulty seeing because of glaucoma.

- Paul Karason turned his skin permanently blue in 1994 after making the mistake of using a home-made remedy. Suffering from dermatitis, he decided to treat the skin complaint himself with his own mix of colloidal silver, an old medicine widely used before the discovery of penicillin. But the silver caused argyria, a condition which turns the skin blue, and it didn't even cure his dermatitis. Irritated by being called 'Papa Smurf' and searching for social acceptance, he eventually left his Oregon home and moved to California, presumably in the hope that Californians, accustomed to weirdness on a daily basis, wouldn't bat an eyelid at seeing a man with a blue face.

- A man from South Kitsap, Washington State, managed to shoot himself in both legs in 2007 while trying to loosen a stiff wheel-nut by firing his rifle at it.

- Jozef Cene, a German police officer, left a Wiltshire pub in 2007 and drove straight into a canal after mistaking it for a wet road. He didn't even have the excuse of being drunk.

- A pair of seventy-eight-year-old burglars were caught red-handed in São Paulo, Brazil, when the homeowners returned unexpectedly. The one inside the house was too deaf to hear the warning of his accomplice outside, and the lookout wasn't fit enough to escape.

What a load of imbeciles.

'An optimist is a guy that has never had much experience.'
Don Marquis

Chapter 18

RANDOM GRUMBLES

- If it's true that we're here to help others, then what exactly are the others here for?

- If practice makes perfect and nobody's perfect, then why practise?

- If swimming is so good for your figure, how come whales are fat?

- Why do they say you've won a free gift? Aren't all gifts free?

- Why is the time of day with the slowest traffic called rush hour?

- Why can't they make an aeroplane out of the same material as the indestructible black box?

- Why is lemon juice made with artificial flavourings yet washing-up liquid is made with real lemons?

- Why is there an expiration date on sour cream?

- How is it that one careless match can start a forest fire, but it takes a whole box to start a campfire?

- Why do toasters always have a setting that burns the bread to a horrible crisp, which no one in their right mind would eat?

- Who came up with the phrase 'quiet as a mouse'? Whoever it was has obviously never stepped on one.

- How come wrong numbers are never busy?

- Why do they always talk about 'the worst floods in living memory' or 'the coldest winter in living memory'? Don't they realize that at our age our 'living memory' goes back to a week last Thursday?

- Why does the website of a charity for the homeless have a home page? That's a bit insensitive, isn't it?

- Why do they call it 'multi-purpose compost' when its only use is for growing plants?

- In court why do they ask if you swear to tell the truth? If you're planning on lying, do they really think you'll tell them so?

- Why do they lock gas station bathrooms? Are they afraid somebody will clean them?

- Why do they never sell car boots at car boot sales?

- If quitters never win and winners never quit, what idiot came up with the saying: 'Quit while you're ahead'?

- Why do mothers take their kids to the supermarket to smack them?

- Why does aspirin come with a childproof cap and yet bullets come in a cardboard box?

- Why do people say, 'It's always in the last place you look'? Of course it is. Why would you keep looking after you've found it?